BEYOND
SURVIVORMAN

LES STROUD

WITH PHOTOGRAPHS BY LAURA BOMBIER

BEYOND
SURVIVORMAN

Collins

Beyond Survivorman

Copyright © 2013 by Stroud Publishing Inc.

All rights reserved.

Published by Collins, an imprint of HarperCollins Publishers Ltd.

First Edition

All photographs, including cover, by Laura Bombier, with the exception of the following by Les Stroud:
pages 16, 18, 20, and 23.

HarperCollins books may be purchased for educational, business, or sales promotional use through our Special Markets Department.

HarperCollins Publishers Ltd
2 Bloor Street East, 20th Floor
Toronto, Ontario, Canada
M4W 1A8

www.harpercollins.ca

Library and Archives Canada Cataloguing in Publication
information is available upon request.

ISBN 978-1-44340-481-5

Printed and bound in Canada

TC 9 8 7 6 5 4 3 2 1

I dedicate this book and my writings to Mother Earth and to the spirit, energy, and power that runs through the planet, our souls, our hearts, and our minds and manifests itself as life. I dedicate this to you the reader, to assimilate in your spirit, in the hopes you will re-manifest your life towards your own happiness and re-invest your physical efforts to honor this planet, by taking yourself to the tipping point of living in a way that protects the earth, not destroys it.

—LS

This book is dedicated to my mother, who moved away from the comforts of the city to raise me in the wilderness of Muskoka—with the sun setting on my face and the water lapping at my feet. To my father, from whom I inherited my travel gene and my insatiable quest for adventure since our first journey together around the time I was 11. And to Les Stroud, who, after my father's sudden death, blessed me with opportunities—too many to count—to capture the amazing cultures, the powerful ceremonies, and the unforgettable experiences that you see in these photographs. "The biggest adventure you can take is to live the life of your dreams." —Unknown

—LB

CONTENTS

Over time and through experience, I have come to understand that keeping a culture alive requires three main components in what I call the cultural triangle: language, land skills, and spirituality. Of these, spirituality is always the most fragile and usually the first to disappear.

Although I often hear about the loss of language from a culture, I find this concern to be a bit of a red herring among anthropologists. Many times I have visited a remotely situated people to find their language alive and well—indicated simply by the fact that nobody speaks English! As for the second side of the triangle, it seems that relatively few lament when land skills are replaced by technology or more modern, "civilized" activities. Rifles replace spears, snowmobiles replace dogsleds, and, most significantly, "jobs" replace life on the land. So although the skills remain much the same, they become modernized. That leaves the spirituality component, often considered quaint according to our supposedly more advanced Western, Judeo-Christian or atheistic standards. Sadly, indigenous cultures appear in danger of losing earth connectedness and animism, two levels of spirituality I believe necessary for the continued health of the earth. And lest we forget, our own existence is intrinsically tied to the health of the earth. The fact is, we breathe out and a tree breathes in; the tree breathes out and we breathe in. Life doesn't get any more connected than that.

None of the stories I tell in this book flies in the face of a spiritual belief in God or scientific belief in atheism (or conflicts with the plethora of other spiritual and non-spiritual human concepts). Whether metaphysical, quantum energy, purely humanistic and physical, God and spirit, or "all in the mind," our beliefs are what they are. If my artistry in whatever I am doing—adventuring, filming, writing, or making music—is not born out of the honesty of what I experience in my life, then I have no business calling myself an artist. Life and the art and truth of living it are bigger than shelters and fire-starting. Life and connecting to the earth are more important than my stories and songs. Of course, none of us will know that for sure until we die or, rather, move on to our next form of life—whatever that may be.

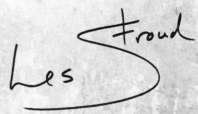

INTRODUCTION

I was at the peak of my career as a documentary filmmaker. I had one of the highest-rated documentary shows on TV. I was getting out of a marriage that was no longer working. I was seeing substantial income for the first time in my life, and I was traveling the world. But two demons combined to make me feel completely lost. The first one was the oppressive thought that I would no longer be with my children a hundred percent of their lives. The second demon made the first one all the more unbearable: I no longer felt I had a deep spiritual connection to the earth. As I lay on the pebble beach on the ocean coast somewhere in Alaska, I couldn't find solace or comfort in the rocks, the trees, the water, the wind, or the clouds—the very elements I'd had a connection with for the previous 15 years of my life. The beauty and the magnificence of the natural world that surrounded me had always sustained me. But it sustained me no more.

I *was* Survivorman. My entire career was based on surviving in the wilderness and that should mean connecting with the wilderness. I wondered, If anyone could "become one with the wilderness" it should be me, shouldn't it? But I had lost it. My time in the wilderness had become a business. It had become a means to an end, when once it was the only end. The wilderness had become a location to create my work, when once it was the work itself. It had become a place of struggle and sometimes suffering, when once it was a place to find relief and rejuvenation. It was becoming my prison, when once it was my freedom.

I began to want that freedom back.

"Les looks like Sting with a degree in edible plants." That's how a journalist described me many years before *Survivorman*, when I was at the peak of my guiding days in Temagami, in northeastern Ontario. A few years before that time, I had walked away from a career in music and television—and my attempts to become a rock star. I was in my late 20s, fit, tanned, and rich in wilderness skills and bush sense. Everything about me had to do with nature and adventure. During every canoe trip, somewhere along the way, I would lie back on a sun-warmed rock and fall asleep looking up at the clouds that danced across the blue sky. In those moments I was a kid again. Nothing else mattered. Not world issues. Not financial issues. Not family issues. Not even romance. (Okay, that always mattered.) Time in the wilderness was a glorious escape from all things domestic, mundane, and tedious. It was a long way from all things big and important to the rest of the world. I could exist completely unaffected by whatever was happening "out there." I was here. Here in the beautiful nature that nurtured my soul. Here where some kind of positive energy force filled me constantly and never brought me down. It was 24/7 nirvana. And it gave me a permanent smile.

Hours would pass as I lay quietly by a lake or river, and then I would turn to one side and kiss that sun-warmed rock beneath me. It was my way of saying thank you. In a similar way, before I would cut down trees to make a survival shelter, I would say thank you to the energy that was about to give of itself to me. When, on any given adventure, I gazed at the glorious splendor that is the natural world, I would say thank you. Thank you to whom or what? I don't really know: God, maybe; Mother Earth, perhaps; the universe itself? I don't know. I knew just that offering gratitude was important because I was truly lucky and blessed to be given all these experiences.

Time and reality marched on. Marriage and kids changed things for the better in many ways. Sue was a strong outdoor tripper, and having her come along on my many adventures let me share nature's gifts with someone I cared for. Even having two kids didn't slow us down at first. We found ways to take them on canoeing and kayaking adventures. But having kids did change one thing: the need to think about the future. And with that came the need to think realistically about money and how it would play into the next 15 or 20 years of our lives. I had been avoiding a lot of these realities. We didn't need much money when we didn't have kids. We traveled the wilderness and loved every minute of it. I always felt very rich and well-off even though my bank account was usually empty. Existence was, and always had been in every sense of the expression, hand to mouth. Most friends we knew, ones who made a far greater yearly income than we did, couldn't get away and have any of the adventures we were able to enjoy. Sue didn't want the adventures to be interrupted by having kids. I wanted kids. But the reality of having them was that even a simple canoe trip would take at least twice as long as it did before. Unless we were willing to become the "rough-around-the-edges hippie family living out in the woods," things would have to change. I was forced to concede that hand-to-mouth existence and living a life of adventure weren't going to work. We considered homesteading and home schooling. I even managed to arrange the purchase of a couple of hundred acres of forested land. But this plan wouldn't be enough.

Perhaps it was because this life with kids forced me to think a lot about owning a home. Perhaps it was because I was no longer able to escape the outside world for months on end like I used to as a guide. But something was gnawing at my soul and at my psyche. It caused me to be unhappy and yearn for more. Something felt like it had been left unattended for far too long. It was my need to create—to be an artist. This is where my music took me once before and I had left it far behind, almost 10 years earlier, to become an adventurer. The only creative endeavor I had undertaken in the past 10 years was making a documentary about the year Sue and I lived in the northern Ontario bush. The film was called *Snowshoes and Solitude*.

After that year of living in the bush, and because Sue came out of that year pregnant, I started taking odd jobs wherever I could get them. Sometimes it was outdoor-related such as teaching survival skills in Yellowknife to Aboriginal people with intellectual disabilities. Sometimes it was painting barge boats in Temagami. And sometimes it was playing small gigs at local pubs for a hundred bucks. So now I had neither the freedom of a life in the woods, which used to consist of canoeing in the summer and running dog teams in the winter, nor the spiritual enjoyment of creative expression through music. My life was all a constant scramble to make enough money to buy diapers and food. And I didn't feel connected to the earth in any way. I began to think of ways to bring back everything that I had lost.

It was about this time that my cousin Peter Dale came into my life. I had been consulting him while I was editing *Snowshoes and Solitude* because he was a professional film editor. When he saw my work and understood my work ethic he made a simple yet life-changing proposition. He offered to fund me for a year at a modest salary to work on more adventure films. This was my ticket, I thought. This was my chance to stay out in the bush and, at the same time, create something meaningful. I would get back my connection to the earth along with a chance to express my passion for creativity through film work and music.

Once again, I would be able to be in a canoe most of the year. Only this time I could take along camera gear and film more of my adventures—and be paid to do so. To keep my family together I came up with the idea of "Wilderness Family." It was a pretty simple concept. I would film our adventures as we traipsed around the northern forests and rivers of Canada. I even had planned a journey that involved sea kayaking the entire coast of the country. Sue was never a leader, while I've always been driven and ambitious. I don't lead a static life. Mine is a life of passion and that always comes with its inherent stresses, while Sue desires a completely stress-free life. And so the cracks in our relationship continued to deepen as the years went by. Sue was always ready and willing to head out, and she was brilliant once she was on the water. But getting there was all me. She loved the journey but not the work it took to organize it. Meanwhile, I was working out of our home. Even my edit suite was in the basement, along with the toddlers and their daily activities. I filmed wildlife and the canoe trips we did as a family and did the editing downstairs. It was an exciting time with lots of promise, but also an intense period with a steep learning curve.

While I was focused on pitching my "Wilderness Family" idea to TV networks, I started getting calls for radio interviews. It seems a new concept show called *Survivor* was making headlines, and the talk shows wanted my take on whether it was real survival. By this time I had built up a reputation as a survival instructor/filmmaker. With all this going on, I dusted off an idea I had had years before. I would offer to head out alone for seven days at a time and film myself surviving. I would bring back a survival odyssey on film. Discovery Channel Canada loved the idea and paid me a small fee to put together the first survival expedition for its signature daily science series called *The Daily Planet*.

I had just returned from the very first film shoot in Northern Ontario when the calendar date turned to September 11, 2001. I immediately called the network people and said I would understand if they wanted to postpone everything, in light of the world-changing circumstances brought about by the attack on the Twin Towers. But they advised me to continue. They were confident that moving forward would be the best thing to do under such horrific circumstances.

When I came back with all my footage, the network had me edit it into five 5-minute segments documenting each of my days of survival. The segments would be aired one day at a time starting on the Monday. By Friday, the network had enjoyed some of its highest ratings in years. It was a hit! I immediately followed up with a winter version, which also did extremely well for the network's daily news and science show. So I took it one step further and offered it as a full-fledged TV series to any network that would listen. OLN in Canada along with the Discovery Channels US and International and the Science Channel gave me the time slot to give it a shot. And the rest, as they say, is history. I now had a full-time job that put me out in the wilderness for adventure, allowed for creative expression, paid the bills, and gave my family and me a chance to see the world.

Ostrich see humans as a threat. One of the greatest dangers I faced while in the Kalahari Desert was going after some ostrich eggs. The males protect the nests, and if they attack, it wouldn't end well for me. With one swipe, an ostrich can split you open from throat to belly, through your rib cage. Its talons are huge, sharp, and lethal.

But I managed to retrieve an egg. One ostrich egg is the equivalent of twenty-four chicken eggs—I snuck it back with me all the way to Canada, cooked it up at home, and served up an egg feast for eight friends!

SURVIVORMAN

I sat on the shore of a remote lake in the early morning mist, completely alone. A couple of days earlier, a crew had dropped me off so I could spend the next seven days filming my survival adventure as part of the TV series I had titled Survivorman. What had I got myself into? So much was riding on my shoulders. I was completely alone. And I felt it. But I didn't feel lonely. I was with the earth again. I was able to feel the breezes, taste the fresh running water, and sit on the energy-filled ground. I turned inside myself. I spoke to the universe. I spoke to God. I spoke to nature. I spoke to whatever force out there would listen.

1

"Whatever it is I am about to do," I said out loud, "please let it be something that will be inspiring and compelling and be a positive influence on people watching." Then I stood up. "Yeah, right," I said under my breath. Who was I kidding? How in the hell can building a bush shelter and showing how to start a fire by rubbing two sticks together end up becoming something "inspirational"? I should give my head a shake, I thought. I turned to walk into the forest and begin my filming. I would start nearly every single day of a *Survivorman* adventure with this kind of spiritual dedication. I didn't know why I did it, other than that I continued to have an inborn need to create something that might have a positive influence on other people. It just felt like the right thing to do.

The process I adopted for filming my *Survivorman* TV series would serve me well in terms of fulfilling a creative goal and taking a good idea to heights I hadn't imagined. But filming the series would also lead me down a road that depleted my own spiritual reserves. I was serving others, or so I hoped, but I would forget to serve myself. I would live and work in some of the most beautiful places on the planet, but I would forget to draw from it the energy and life-giving force I needed to fill my soul. The business of *Survivorman* would take over and distract me for enough years to empty my spiritual bank account. Disillusionment, betrayal, and divorce were around the corner. I couldn't see them coming.

The modest and humble approach to filming *Survivorman* always remained at the core of my creative outflow. But the peripheral circumstances changed rapidly. When I filmed the very first version for *The Daily Planet,* I was paid $11,000 to produce the entire work, start to finish (and it took a year), and I was happy to get it. By the second season of *Survivorman,* I had managed to up the budget to nearly $300,000 an episode. This figure included helicopter aerial shots to put extra footage into the show for beauty shots. It meant a business partner and editors and production staff. The first two versions of *Survivorman* were done almost entirely by me in my basement: the music, the editing, the color correction, the audio mix—everything. Now I had a team. I had staff. I had responsibilities.

But back out on the expeditions, I had nature all to myself again. I was able to see the natural splendor of far flung corners of the world. And I had my introduction to learning from indigenous peoples: men, women, and children who live on and with the land; people who love and respect the land; and those who know that nature is the source of their lives and live accordingly. I was humbled by them. But I was busy. I had shots to get, a story to go out and shoot. In the second season I had to film nine straight episodes. That meant surviving somewhere without food and water for seven days at a time, nine times in a year. Physically speaking, that was ludicrous. No survival expert or instructor would do that. But I had signed contracts. The series was a hit and it was making the networks a lot of money. So I had no time to roll over and kiss the rock I was sleeping on. I had no time to thank the spirits of the land for letting me survive there. I was a filmmaker with a hit TV series to film. But one thing remained constant—I never forgot to ask the powers that be to guide me into making something that inspired people in a positive way. In many strange and wonderful ways my request was heard and, it would seem, acted on.

One day I read an e-mail I could barely get through. A woman told me that her daughter had been brutally raped and murdered a year before. For the entire year, the grieving mother had lived in darkness, believing there was no one and nothing good in this world. Then she saw my show. She said it gave her her first breath of fresh air since the horrific tragedy. I cried as I read her note. Then more e-mails came in. One was from a father who said my show gave him and his estranged son something to connect through and led to a renewed relationship. Another was from a man who said the show got him through eight months in a hospital bed. Still another, from a young woman with a newborn, said the show helped pull her out of an abusive relationship. The mail kept arriving. I was astounded. I was humbled. Somehow, those little prayers or meditations—whatever you want to call them—that I said at the beginning of every shooting day of *Survivorman*, somehow they worked. Somehow, a little show about shelters and fires was inspiring people and even changing lives. In the midst of a very nasty TV business, I was reassured and given hope by people who had experienced my work. This response helped a lot. But it wasn't enough.

The din of the business of TV was loud enough to drown out the positive voices of people who were watching my shows. And it kept growing louder. It drowned out the voice of the wilderness that was trying to communicate with me, through my time in its remote places and with the people who lived there. It even threatened to drown out my own sense of creativity.

I remained doing what I do and tried to stay true to the core of what I started in the first place, but the effort took its toll on me. I thought I had got into this adventure so I could be close to nature. I thought the idea was that I could be out in the wilderness and create something worthwhile and make money at the same time. But now I had become a businessman. I was actually good at reading a contract and understanding it well enough to debate it, and that was never a skill I wanted to become good at. I wasn't even very fit anymore. I started flying first class, and my ticket price for appearances or hosting other shows (*Shark Week*, for example) went up big time.

It should have been that, when I found myself back on a *Survivorman* shoot, I would be filled with positive energy; that I would communicate with nature and replenish my spiritual reserves. But it wasn't happening. My marriage was falling apart. Sue could never get on board this new train. I needed her help to organize the business, the house, and the kids. I needed her to help us keep the nature in our family endeavors. But her passion wasn't there, no matter how much she said she loved our life together. I just couldn't do it all: argue contracts, film *Survivorman*, host other shows, run an office and staff, organize nature trips for our family, and keep myself spiritually grounded with the love of my life—the earth itself—all at the same time.

Eight years into making *Survivorman* shows, I needed to move on. I needed to find a new creative outlet. Something I could grow with again. Something I could put my passion into. But, most important, I needed to find my way back into a relationship with the earth. I needed to understand its rhythms again. I wanted to feel its nuances and subtleties once more. My creativity needed it. My body needed it. My soul needed it. I wondered where to find the connection I had lost. I wondered who could help me get back in touch with nature.

I stood on a walkway overlooking a street somewhere in Phoenix, Arizona. Fresh from filming season three of *Survivorman*, I knew the networks wanted either many more episodes . . . or something new. But what was it? What that I had not yet experienced would whet my appetite? *Survivorman* was a hard act to follow. Indeed, all the attempts to copy it by my own and other networks could only fake it. How could I progress and do something different?

I realized my quest was to connect with the last of the world's remaining remote tribes and earth-based cultures, to survive with them in the wild, to take part in their ceremonies, and to partake of their plant medicines to deepen my connection with the earth. Out of these experiences new questions would emerge and perhaps be answered. Is it possible to take the lessons from the remote earth cultures and use them to heal the disharmony in our societies? Can we learn from the last indigenous people how to regain the balance of a natural, sustainable life on this planet? Can we get past their primitive appearance and learn from them how to survive into the next century?

After years of filming *Survivorman,* I felt I had lost touch with Mother Earth and who she truly was. You would think that, given my work, I would be—in the fullest sense of the cliché—"one with nature." But I wasn't. I had been so caught up in the business of producing a television series that I felt disconnected from the spirit of the earth. I wanted my connection back.

I saw this new series—which was to be called *Les Stroud: Beyond Survival*—as a fantastic exploration, but I was to get more than I bargained for. Before my year producing *Beyond Survival* was over, I would gain a spiritual understanding I didn't know I could achieve. I knew I would change and learn, but I did not know to what extent. Hell, part of me was just trying to figure out the meaning of life. I wondered if such introspection and spiritual exploration would turn my face away from the spotlight of celebrity and toward a self-imposed exodus from it all.

I was ready for something that grew beyond survival shelters and hunting with a bow and arrow. Don't get me wrong: I knew what people enjoyed about my survival work, and I would make sure to pay homage to it. But I needed to go farther, reach higher. And I needed to get back in touch with myself and with the earth.

So, like I always do, I jumped headfirst into the unknown. I had trust and faith that I could handle whatever befell me, that it would all be part of living life to the fullest extent. And besides, I wanted to make history . . . or at least document it. Let the copycats pretend to be survival heroes. I had bigger fish to fry.

But a small voice of skepticism lurked deep inside me. What if I learned nothing? What if I was too hardheaded to experience anything? I am not easily hypnotized, if at all. I am not one to fall down speaking in tongues at the drop of a preacher's hat. I see things as they are. I am a realist. I need proof. I need understanding. I need more than just emotional euphoria. What if all I could manage was simply to film my survival and a few ceremonies? What if all I really was about was shelters and fire bows?

Enter South Africa.

Eating scorpions is the epitome of getting over "plate fright" (as I described it in *Survive! Essential Skills and Tactics to Get You Out of Anywhere Alive*). In some deserts you need to turn over a lot of rocks to find them, but in the Kalahari all you need do is bury a jar without a top at the base of their hole during the day. Overnight, as they crawl out, they fall into your jar. I caught many with this simple and effective trap.

Once you have removed all the stingers and have skewered the scorpions shish-kebab style, you are left with a squirming collection of creepy crawlies ready to roast—a very unsightly meal that will turn most stomachs. Like grasshoppers, however, scorpions cook up quickly, taste nearly like little crispy shrimp, and provide a tiny boost of protein.

WATER IS THE ELIXIR OF LIFE—IT IS THE ENERGY THAT FLOWS THROUGH OUR PLANET. I HAVE A TRADITION: WHENEVER I COME TO A NEW PLACE, I SEEK OUT A STREAM TO DRINK FROM DIRECTLY. I GET DOWN ON MY HANDS AND KNEES AND TAKE IN THE WATER WITH THE INTENT OF FEELING CONNECTED TO THE PLACE, AND I FEEL THE LIFE-GIVING ENERGY OF THE WATER AS IT QUENCHES MY THIRST. I KNOW THAT FROM THAT MOMENT ON I WILL ALWAYS HAVE A CONNECTION TO THE LAND BECAUSE THE ENERGY THAT FLOWS WITHIN IT AND KEEPS IT ALIVE IS NOW FLOWING WITHIN ME.

2

DIVINE HEALERS

The Sangoma

Basing the decision on a combination of logistics, schedules, and budgets, my production manager had to pinpoint the locations I would be sent off to as well as when I would go. As filming began, I prepared myself for a season of location shoots crisscrossing the globe. My itinerary was, effectively, random. Or so I thought.

The first location shoot for the new series was in South Africa with the Zulu. I selected my remote locations according the cultures that had a good combination of land-based survival methods they still used, as well as deep and meaningful ceremonies that connected them with the land.

I was most interested in the Zulu scarification ceremony. This film shoot provided a mixed bag of opportunities, among them attending a traditional Zulu wedding, taking part in a stick fight, and chasing down a couple of deadly snakes. The biggest hope of the shoot rested on dog hunting. What we were going to hunt for I was never quite sure. I believe it was basically anything the dogs might scare up in front of us: African deer, birds, or any assortment of rodents. So early in the morning somewhere out in the mist where two dirt roads met, we gathered about 15 local hunters and a few dogs.

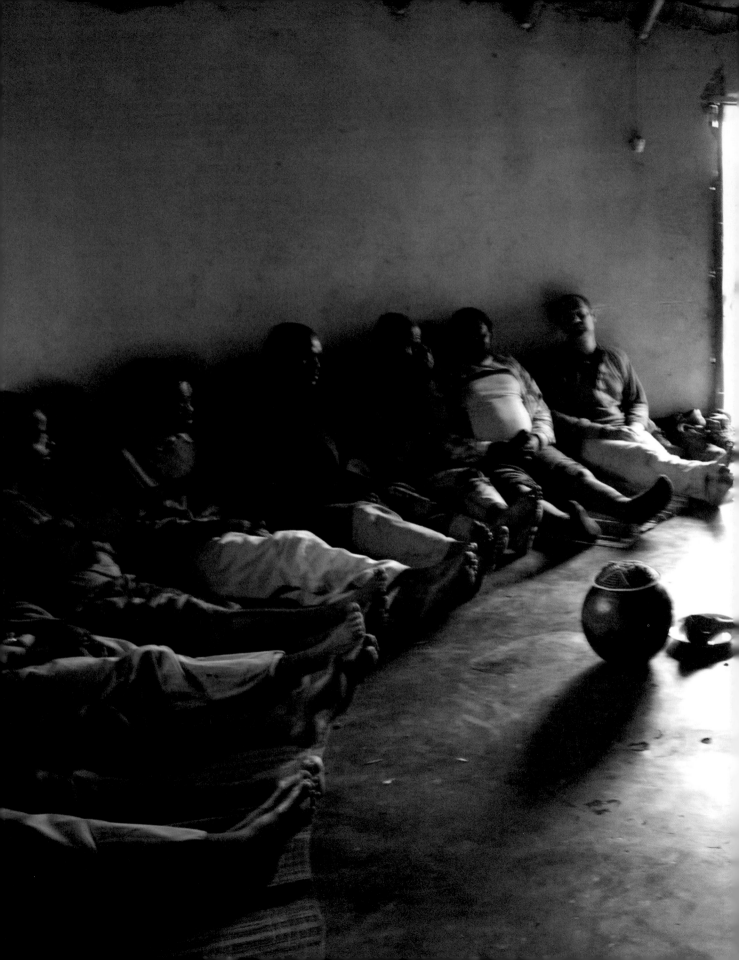

Short ceremonies were carried out to help us in the hunt and bring us luck. Then off we all went through the dry shrub brush and trees, always listening intently for the dogs to start barking. We had a small valley to hunt in, bordered by a cliff and the roads. If anything came running out at us, we would have a great chance of capturing it or hitting it with throwing sticks. Throwing sticks are basically small clubs. If the dogs went crazy, you knew they were on to something. About four hours of trekking through the land went by without a single bit of action. We pushed hard, trying to follow the dogs that were chasing after a million different scents.

This is black mamba territory—home to a notoriously dangerous snake that can grow to 15 feet long, stand up as tall as half its body length, and out-slither a man running in a hundred-yard stretch. With thoughts of mamba in my head, I found myself climbing over vines and crawling on my belly underneath thick shrubbery. Other than my stops to learn about some healing plants, the day was quickly becoming a bust. As I crawled through yet another tangle I heard the call that the hunt needed to be stopped. It took me another 15 minutes to make it to the leaders. I had to slither along the ground with my face close to the dry, hard earth while pushing through tall grass. Because of the curled brush overhead, I was unable to stand up. It was like an African *Pan's Labyrinth*. Apparently we had walked ourselves right into what was most likely the one spot with the greatest density of black mambas, during a peak time of mamba activity. Their trails, I was told, were through the tall grass and thick shrubbery in which I had just spent a good hour facedown. Sometimes it's good not to know what you've got yourself into until you're out of it! Thankful to be free and clear of any attacks by one of the most aggressive and poisonous snakes on the planet, I was more excited to get back to the small village where I was to take part in a divine healing ceremony.

Sangoma is what they called her. It means "divine healer" in the Zulu language of South Africa. She would be the first stop on my journey to the center of me. She looked surprisingly young, given her status in the community, but there was wisdom of a thousand years in her eyes. Her hair was in beaded dreadlocks and she wore the colorful, flowing clothing of her people. She spoke quietly and softly, almost in a whisper, her voice as gentle and soothing as her demeanor. Her hands were dark and ancient looking. She had the kind of look, the kind of smile, that instantly reassured you, that let you know she was there with your best interests at heart. The perfect combination of innocent child and wise elder, Sangoma looked like she was there to protect your very soul for you.

People came to Sangoma for many reasons: because of a physical sickness or mental illness, to seek out where and when good hunting should happen, even to reconnect with their ancestors. As we approached the dry and dusty grouping of thatched huts halfway up the hillside on a parched landscape, we paused to carry out the Zulu tradition of calling from a distance before entering the yard. The tradition is a throwback to when attacks from enemy tribes could happen at any time. The enemy would sneak up; your friends wouldn't. Sangoma led me into a tiny hut, where we all settled—the camera crew awkwardly organizing itself for such a powerful spiritual event. A handful of her younger family members, holding drums and shakers, also filed into the hut and sat down. They were much more reserved, not looking the visitors in the face but happy to do Sangoma's bidding.

I had heard about scarification, a process that is as much a rite of passage among the Zulu and other tribes as it is a way to associate you with your family clan. I had even seen it in some documentary films: young men lie grimacing on the ground while razor blades are drawn across their bellies in a series of long, bloody lines. I wanted to experience it myself because it looked powerful. It looked painful, too, but I felt I could handle it. It seemed like a potent rite of passage. Scarification was also the process by which I would henceforth always be accepted as a member of the Zulu people.

Smudging and other preparations were administered as I sat in the hut. I could sense something stirring within me that a year later would not only feel familiar, but also define my purpose in life. It was this feeling of straddling a knife-edge and existing as two minds. One part of me was relaxed with Sangoma's gentle preparations while trying to feel a spiritual awakening. The other looked at the camera on the ground and tried to maneuver it into a good position for the shot I needed. It bothered me. How could I become one with this ceremony while the camera crew was trying to capture it all on film? Yes, they were respectful and quiet, but a huge distraction to me nonetheless. I had to learn how to filter them out of my consciousness, and it was not going to be easy. Yet how else could I be a filmmaker at the same time tasked with creating something compelling to experience, watch, and enjoy?

For the Zulu, scarification, still important today, is a form of tattooing that brings a youth into adulthood, distinguishes a family clan, or just helps beautify the body. But Sangoma had other plans for me. She told me that I was on a great journey and that the scars she would give me were for spiritual protection. The markings were to be visible to scare off the malevolent spirits and attract the protective ones, who would know that I was to be looked after.

Not one drop of my blood was allowed to fall on the ground or be left behind, so Sangoma's gentle, warm, and caring hands dabbed the blood trickling down my temples and forehead after she gently pinched and cut into them. She collected the bloodied gauze in a little bit of newspaper. The Zulu once used sharp rocks to cut the skin, but they now have the luxury of razor blades. (Because of the huge impact of AIDS, she uses only sterile blades.) I tried hard to surrender emotionally, mentally, and spiritually. Yet my voices of reason and intellect were strong and they tried hard to drown out the voices of my heart and soul. It is thought that when reason and ego run the soul, the heart cannot truly live.

Sangoma giggled and pointed out that I was sweating with nervousness. She reassured me to relax. She cut me some more, in marks of three on my temples, forehead, and the back of my neck. Strangely, I felt almost nothing. All my anxiousness about the pain I thought I might feel was unwarranted. She gently pinched my skin to take the feeling out while she administered one-inch slices with the blade to make the marks. I could feel the warmth of my blood trickle down my face. She said because I am a man, *and because of the great journey that she was convinced I was about to take,* I would need protection from all sides. So I also received scars on the top, bottom, and sides of my back.

She then rubbed charcoal powder deep into the cuts, turning them into a tattoo that will not fade with age. I hadn't really felt much of the cutting. However, when she applied the charcoal powder, I thought she was rubbing salt into a wound. The charcoal marks, the Zulu believe, will protect me from acts of witchcraft.

Afterward, we danced and chanted. Sangoma's bright, powerful, shrill voice rose and wavered above the hut, a primordial sound that cut through my spine. Cloaked in a colorful robe, I danced and sang with her. Her ankles and mine were adorned with noisemakers made with a combination of natural items and the lids of soda pop cans. The hut was crammed with her young assistants playing drums and chanting in the South African heat. Though I didn't realize it at the time, we were singing ancient African melodies that would be an inspiration to me a year later as I crafted material for a music tour. None of the family members looked like they were playing a role for the white visitor. They seemed serious and focused on the importance of this ceremony. It was clear that their respect for Sangoma was very high.

After we finished, Sangoma told me to leave the hut and not look back or I might give the spirits that had been banished from me a chance to follow and return to me. She instructed me to take my spilled blood and bury it along with the razor blades, to leave behind the evil spirits. I climbed a nearby hill to find a small spot where I could bury the gauze and razors. For me the burial represented a very deep way of leaving a part of me in Africa.

Now it was time for celebration. I met the crew back in another house. I sat with the men of the village and stood up like they did, one at a time, to dance an African dance to great cheers from dozens of men and women crammed into a large building. The building itself had no one living in it. It was built and exists for such occasions but primarily serves as a domicile for the "ancients"—those who have passed on. Imagine it. They actually maintain a building to house their deceased ancestors—beautiful. We all drank from a large bowl of Zulu beer—brewed at home by village women—that was passed around for the elders and for me, their new family member. My time in Africa, however, was not over.

3

ANCIENTS CALL

The San Bushmen

The San Bushmen are making their last stand in the Kalahari Desert. Small groups of these sun-scorched people exist in Namibia, a beautiful country situated just north of Botswana and South Africa on the west coast of the continent. They are being displaced and assimilated at a rapid pace. As is so often the case, the government considers these aboriginal people a speed bump on the road to "progress," which usually means exploiting the environment for profit. As a result, only a few San remain, hunting with poison arrows, carrying water in ostrich eggs when they travel, and living in small grass huts. The elders see the changes coming, and as it is in many other indigenous cultures around the world, the San, at least the older generations, are upset by the loss of their traditional ways. They are saddened that their youth will not know the land and its ways the way they do. The youth will get jobs. They will do deliveries and sit in cubicles instead of walking under the scorching sun in the desert lands catching rodents or large game or digging for roots. But culture, by its very nature, changes constantly and sometimes rapidly.

People like the San were left well enough alone until 50 years ago. Now they don't stand a chance at escaping the crosshairs of the rifle of progress. Cell phones and SUVs quickly replace sign language and walking, even if geography keeps the people "out on the land." But what else should we expect? The San, like so many others, cannot be kept in a petrified state of their own traditional culture while we remain "voyeurs" looking in on our human ant farm to see how it's doing. We don't live like our grandparents. Why would we expect the San to? Yet the greatest lament I often hear comes from middle-aged parents who love their own land-based skill set and are dismayed that their children are distracted and uninterested. But along with cell phones come computers and thus the Internet, which serves to introduce them to the greatest cultural steamroller of all: the outside world and its tantalizing and increasingly homogenized global culture. To the youth, their spirituality and land-based skill set becomes outdated and quaint.

Ironically, the San exist only a short jeep ride from resorts, the same resorts that provide them with supplies in return for their ostrich egg necklaces and other handmade trinkets. Not surprisingly, given their proximity to modernized areas, some San villages resemble human petting zoos, where tourists pull up in buses to watch the sacred trance dances. None of the Bushmen are "un-contacted." They know white people, and they know vehicles. They know about towns, roads, and other modern amenities. They sit in small circles in their marginalized little villages, making trinkets to sell. A traveler from the outside world could once find beautiful artifacts that were actually used by people who live on the land. Now what one buys at a roadside market almost anywhere in Africa was made to be sold—and only to be sold. Gone are the days of extraordinary and authentic domestic creations. Still, some San remain on the land, steadfastly holding on to whatever vestiges of their traditional lifestyle they can. These are the Bushmen I was seeking out.

One of my first activities with the San was, typically, hunting on the land. This time it would require a long hike—them in their leathery bare feet, me in heavy hiking boots, and all of us passing through the hot, dry, scorched, and prickly desert lands of Namibia in search of porcupine; or, to be more direct, in search of porcupine holes with the hope that the beasts themselves would be inside. Whenever I went out on a hunting expedition during the filming of *Beyond Survival* I would go alone, without my camera crew. Anyone who hunts knows it is virtually impossible to do so with a large group of noisy men clambering through the area. Alone with experts such as these Bushmen, we could swiftly and quietly cut through the bush. My challenge of course was carrying my own camera gear and capturing anything exciting the moment it happened. My other challenge was attempting to walk as quietly as they did in my big clunky hiking boots.

It was opportunistic hunting. If my companions sensed anything along the way—a kudu (a large antelope), perhaps—the movement and sounds we were making would come to a quick stop and we'd focus on getting downwind from a small herd of beasts. The small poison-tipped arrows and bows of the San hunters would immediately be raised in anticipation of getting a shot at a large ungulate. We were not successful at this venture but managed to gather up a few small land turtles for turtle soup later on. My cohorts spoke no English and I'm a little rusty on the clicks and pops of the San language, so we never uttered a word. Even among themselves, talking was almost nonexistent. As we traversed the brown landscape we constantly came on old porcupine holes. Large and deep, extending as far as 50 feet underground, the holes, covered as they were by massive spider webs (probably made by tarantulas), were obviously old. Every once in a while I'd be cautioned to be careful because leopards would often hide in them from the midday sun but wouldn't hesitate to jump out and attack.

At last we saw some fresh porcupine tracks, then some more, and then, finally, a lot of tracks, all heading in one direction. We followed these markings in the dirt to a large mound with multiple holes on each end. We had to move fast. The porcupines would hear our feet on the ground and would escape to the farthest place underground they could get to. But this trick wouldn't hold back the Bushmen, who immediately started digging at one end of the hole so that they could climb down and squirm through the tiny underground tunnel in the dark to get to the animals.

I couldn't believe what I saw. The Bushmen had warned me before we left on the hunt that more than once a hunter has been buried alive this way. At one point I handed the man going down in the hole my small camera with night vision so he could look ahead of himself in the tunnel and find the porcupine. At the other end of the tunnel, one Bushman and I stood with spears in our hands waiting for the porcupine to come running out in an attempt to escape. When it finally happened all hell broke loose. Not one but two massive quill-covered and very angry porcupines came out of the hole and were soon stuck with a spear and held to the ground until death. It was a very intense moment. The animals let out a blood-curdling cry as their life left them. The San actually began to smile. The two porcupines would feed the village tonight.

Before we could carry the animals back to the village, they had to be burned externally to kill off numerous ticks and bugs and then cut up for dispersal among the men. In addition, this catch meant a well-deserved and needed meal for the hunters. But first they had to start a fire. I smiled broadly when I saw the eldest pull out a traditional tiny hand drill to start the fire. No matches. What was so astounding about this moment was that it conveyed a modern-day use of what is likely the very first method of fire-starting by humans being carried out by what are believed to be the very first line of the human species: the San Bushmen. Tonight they would enjoy the feast of porcupine, and tomorrow I would travel to another group of Bushmen to take part in their traditional ceremonies of connecting with their ancestors.

Only once a year they gather honey from one massive hive within miles of the village.

As I approached the small village of Bushmen known to be healers and trance dancers, my first impression was disturbing. It was my own fault, really, since I expected to find them looking like the stereotypes that were well developed in my brain. We always set ourselves up for disappointment when we have preconceived notions of how someone or something is supposed to look or act—it's like a blind-date letdown. Instead of wearing loincloths and carrying spears, these men were farmers with cattle and chickens. Worse yet, they were very accustomed to performing their trance dances for tourists who visit only for an hour or so, then return to their scotches and cappuccinos at a lodge a two-hour drive away. I needed more. I needed to know if these trance dancers were for real. Do they perform the dances whether outsiders have come or not? Do they dress up when they perform the dances on their own? Do they still really enter trances? And what was their purpose for it all? Could I fall into a trance?

PEOPLE OFTEN ASK ME why these remote cultures accept me so readily. My two-pronged approach is fairly simple. First, I offer food and supplies to show my gratitude for allowing me to come into their community. Then I ask my hosts to look into my eyes and heart and decide for themselves if they think I can be trusted. If they don't like what they see, they can send me home.

Yet as comfortable as I am with this approach, there's always some trepidation. After all, it usually costs me hundreds of thousands of dollars to make these experiences happen for the purpose of filming a television series. If I fly halfway around the world with a camera crew, only to be sent packing, I would have a lot of explaining to do back home. But I try to assure my hosts that my presence is about me connecting with them. I tell them to think of the crew as flies buzzing around. They are to share with me and teach me, to show me the beauty of their culture.

Our translator walked me into the circle of dark, wrinkled, and leathery smiling faces: the shamans and their wives. Other men, women, and children from the village gathered around to meet me and learn about my visit. At first, the feeling was one of distrust. They were accustomed simply to performing their dances, selling some crafts, and letting the tourists leave. Why did I require a special meeting with the shaman?

So I told them: I didn't want them to do for me what they do for outsiders. If they don't wear costumes when they dance on their own, then don't wear them for me. Teach me how to trance. Show me the hard-core experience as much as possible. In return I would stay and learn for three days without quitting. They thanked me for my small gift of rice and a few supplies and then paused to consider what I had said. They told me that trance dancing is difficult. I would be driven to exhaustion. They told me that I would have to stick with it, and not relent, all day and into the night. I showed them that I accepted their warnings by nodding and agreeing. My interpreter made it very clear to them I wasn't the usual tourist—that I longed for something deep. Then they smiled and accepted my request.

The San believe their trance dance is an opportunity for the souls of the living to journey through space and time to the world of the ancients, where wisdom and insight are passed on. The purpose of the trance is to gain insight and healing by journeying to the spirit world and connecting to the ancients, the true masters of survival. It is called "half death." The spirit of the trance dancer actually departs on a visionary journey to the spirit world to acquire knowledge by communing with the ancients. Modern, civilized man (at least this one) has lost that ability. I was hoping the San could teach me the methods of trancing and restore that ability.

Yet questions raced through my mind. Was this a simple method, and all they had to do was teach me? Would it require plant medicine or some kind of repetitive motion that would hypnotize me? Was it accomplished through exhaustion? I wasn't sure how they could give me this ability, but I hoped they could at least point me in the right direction by teaching me the dance.

And that, I am sure, is exactly how they saw it. They would direct and guide me, but the results were up to me and might not be evident for months—or years—to come. All I had to do was remain open. I really didn't know what to look for or expect. I had never *seen* the spirit world. The San would go into the trance and work hard to put spirits into me that would keep me strong. They would work hard to connect me to the ancients. They told me the ancients would be willing to talk to me if I was willing to dance.

The women sat around a fire on the dry and dusty ground peppered with cow patties. One started chanting and clapping; the rest joined in and didn't stop for hours at a time. Even though I am a musician, their rhythm was difficult to discern at first. (It's is actually a rhythm known as an African six.) The men circled the women with short, heavy stamping. The decorative rattles on the men's ankles—a collection of seed pods, tin cans, and plastic—pulsed and stressed each beat. Dust stirred up from the ground, creating a misty-looking haze in the hot African air.

The other men and I hunched forward with our arms close to our sides. Two shamans, two young men, and I made up the circling group. Often, one of the elder women jumped up in a state of frenzy and stepped in front of me. She then placed my hands on her shoulders and led me around the ring of fire circling the clapping, chanting women. This act made me feel warm and accepted. There was emotion in her touch, caring in her moves, and a closeness to me that was palpable. She was old and strong and seemed to have the experience of a few thousand trance dances within her. The men were tightly flexed, waiting to fall into a trance. Ultimately, the women's singing and clapping brought the group to so heated a frenzy that the San describe it as an energy boiling up their spinal columns and into their heads. The women's singing was shrill and otherworldly. As the spirit of the men rose it overcame them. The men lost themselves to the trance.

One of the men in the circle had only one arm. Years before, distraught over the fact that he had beaten up another man, he punished himself by stabbing his own arm with a poison arrow. Many days later he recovered in the hospital, though his poisoned arm had been amputated. This day, sheer physical exhaustion and the heat of the day sent him into a trance. He collapsed to the dusty ground, his eyes rolled back in his head. The lead shaman held the man's head up and chanted into his body. Both men quivered.

Later I would be told that the man had been trance dancing for years, but this was his first successful deep trance. Indeed, until today he was a shaman in training like an apprentice; I was there to witness him reaching full shaman status. It can take years to master the trance journeying. The dancers took my interest seriously and felt they did not want to let me down in teaching their great skill of going into the trance journey. When the trance happens, a man's body feels indestructible. He can walk through fire and rub hot coals against his body, sometimes receiving horrific burns but seemingly with no pain whatsoever.

Dancing with them was exhausting, and the heat of the desert so intense I felt the physical strains . . . but not the spiritual ones. Doubts swirled in my mind, if only for a moment. I didn't expect to go into a trance, but I wished I could. I knew it was something that could take years to achieve. But every movement I made, the hundreds of times I circled the relentlessly chanting and clapping women, was carried out with respect, dignity, and a desire to feel something.

Again, that familiar feeling appeared. I was stomping, breathing, going into myself and focusing. All the while I could see the camera crew out of the corner of my eye. Were they getting this shot properly? Were they being respectful of these trance dancers? Were they ruining the experience for the San? One photographer asked me to move a bit to the side for a better angle; my glare let him know I was not to be interrupted.

The dance went on into the night: hours and hours, one foot in front of the other, around and around on the hot desert sand underneath a black and star-filled sky. The San marked my skin with charcoal. They rubbed my body with their hands and their heads, while screaming into my belly and reaching into my heart: trying to put good spirits into me; trying to connect me with the ancients. The women never stopped. Their endurance seemed beyond human. I felt lost in the heat and sweat and eerie singing.

The San explained that they were greatly honored to have someone take such a deep interest in their vanishing practice. So they focused their interest on me. They wanted to teach me. They put spirits into me through touch and voice, rubbing me and yelling into my stomach to chase out the demons. They showed me the path and left it to me to venture down it, so I could continue my journey and use their teaching in my world. The wisdom of the ancients knows no political or geographical boundaries, they said. The ancients are always present—ready to be accessed, ready to impart knowledge. But only if I seek them out.

The San connect to the spirit world to seek knowledge, to appease the spirits, and to find out where to hunt, where to live, and how to survive. I, too, tried to connect with the ancients as they showed me their way. I saw nothing and heard nothing but the African chanting, the hand clapping and rattle shaking and the crackling of the fire.

But I heard the echo of Sangoma in my heart: *You are on a great journey.* So it seemed this was step number two of that journey. It seemed that the arbitrary scheduling of these location shoots and ceremonies by my production manager might have some kind of predetermined direction that I had not actually planned.

It's said that in North America the porcupine is one of the safest meals you can eat in a survival situation. In fact, you can eat them raw with very little worry of disease. The biggest problem I have with the spiny little guys is that when they're trapped, scared, injured, or otherwise stressed, they unleash a scream that sounds way too much like a bawling human baby! The Kalahari porcupines were no different. Their cries of terror as the bushmen speared them when they tried to escape their hole were so bad that I didn't include them during my filming of the San Bushman episode. If there is one thing I don't have the stomach for, it's dispatching game in the name of survival while they let out hair-raising, agonizing cries. Survival takes more than just knowing some good bush skills. The spirit of the animal may have been willing to give up its body for your feast and your survival, but the body is often not so willing!

4

GYPSIES OF THE SEA

The Sea Bajau

After going through scarification in South Africa and trance dancing in the Kalahari Desert, I felt I was on my way toward a spiritual shift. Though my journey was not without struggle, the ceremonies were deep, mysterious, and captivating, and I could feel my heart opening, if only a little.

Yet my doubt and skepticism remained. Although the scarification ceremony was emotionally touching, I never felt like more than a simple recipient of protection and blessings, which seemed nice enough. Even with the trance dance, where I was very much a participant—stomping and sweating long hours into the African nights—I never went into any kind of trance or even had a special feeling. It was fascinating to be sure, even compelling. But I heard no voices. I didn't talk to the ancients. I suppose I shouldn't be so hard on myself. I was told I wouldn't trance, anyway. It takes years to achieve that level, and I had only three days, no matter how concentrated they were.

The ability to see beyond our everyday physical realm has always fascinated me. But it is with a skeptic's eye that I watch and seek out such experiences. What if, in the end, it's all poppycock? What if all the magic and otherwise inexplicable occurrences that people bear witness to are just a collection of incredible coincidences and hallucinations? What if our physical reality is nothing more than a blip in a universe far bigger and more powerful than we can ever know with our human minds? Are we spirits inhabiting physical form for a brief period or just—as an alien character in *Men in Black* called us—pond scum? And what of all these earth energies I keep hearing about? What of quantum physics?

These kinds of questions wrestled with my growing openness to learn as I continued on my journey. This time I would fly halfway around the world to learn from people who live close to and even within the ocean: the Sea Bajau.

The Sea Bajau people, or Sea Gypsies as they are often called (I use both terms interchangeably in this chapter), live on, and in, the ocean. Their environment is like the set of the movie *Waterworld*; only the gills are missing. These are a displaced people. They have no country, no rights. In fact, they have no land. They exist only by living on the ocean near the thousands of tiny islands peppered throughout the sea, in a combination of spindly stick huts and small boats. Yet as bizarre as this arrangement may seem, the Sea Bajau actually prefer it that way. They go to the land and collect only water, coconuts, and wood for small fires aboard their boats. And that's just for a few minutes on any given day.

To the Sea Bajau, the ocean is the mother of all life; they carry her energy within themselves. It is believed they came from the southern Philippines and have lived this way for over two hundred years. A peaceful people, they spend their time in temporary locations as conditions permit, pulling up anchor and paddling or motoring away to another unnamed spot near another unnamed island.

There are actually three economic groupings among the Sea Bajau. Those in the top rung belong to Sea Gypsies who have managed to use Asian markets to create some form of financial foundation for their lives, which ultimately means larger boats. They're still pretty rough-looking boats, but they are big enough to support a dozen or so people. These are what you might consider the "elite" Sea Gypsies, were such a thing possible.

The members of the next group keep small boats but prefer to live in tiny stick huts only feet from an island shore. They are literally a stone's throw from actual (recognized) Malaysians who live in huts *attached* to the shore, but they don't associate much with each other except to pass while collecting freshwater from the only well on the island. This subset of Sea Bajau often harbors desires to build *on* the island itself. But these people don't dare, as either the government or land-based Malaysians would quickly run them out.

The last subset includes those who live only in tiny boats big enough to handle four or five people, but that often hold as many as eight. They want nothing of the land or living on it (coconuts, water, and wood seem to be all they really need from the land); they prefer life on the waves. It was with this last group that my journey with the Sea Bajau began.

My host, Maxiludin, shared his wooden-hulled boat with his wife and his son, who looked to be about 6 or 7 years old. Their boat was cramped yet colorful, thanks to the various tarps that provided both shade and rain protection. The family got everything they needed from the sea, including floating garbage. Sadly, floating garbage is always readily at hand, so many of their meager possessions were made from plastic jugs and the like. The casing for the motor itself was a white bleach bottle.

Maxiludin's family did not speak a word of English. Surprisingly, I found this to be a great advantage, since it forced me to develop an intimate set of hand and eye signals with my hosts, which resulted in our becoming close.

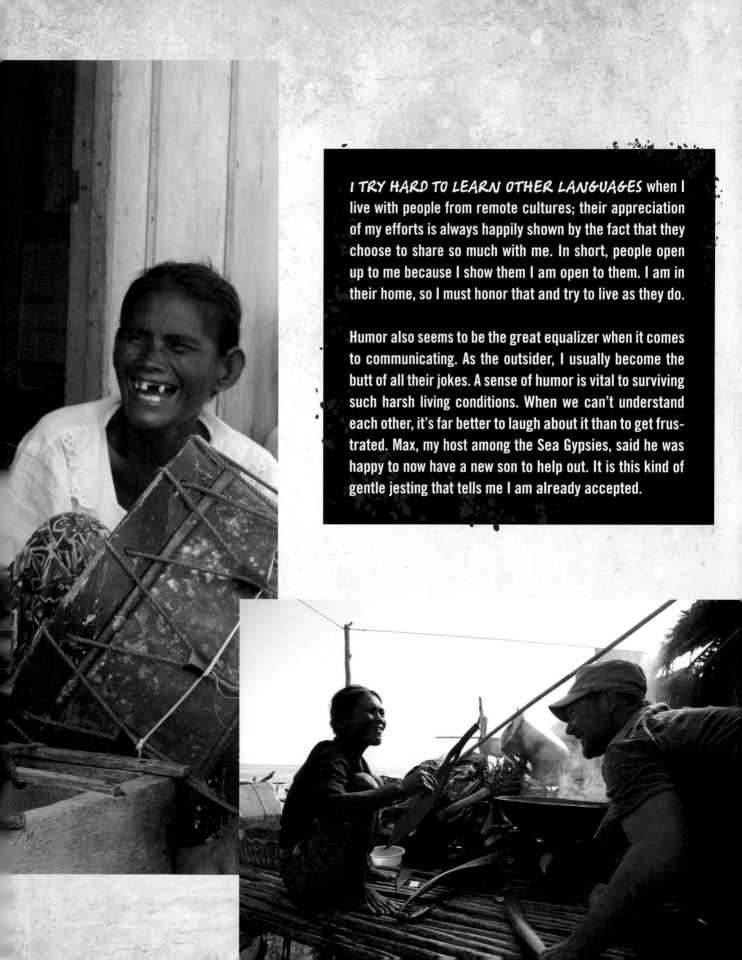

I TRY HARD TO LEARN OTHER LANGUAGES when I live with people from remote cultures; their appreciation of my efforts is always happily shown by the fact that they choose to share so much with me. In short, people open up to me because I show them I am open to them. I am in their home, so I must honor that and try to live as they do.

Humor also seems to be the great equalizer when it comes to communicating. As the outsider, I usually become the butt of all their jokes. A sense of humor is vital to surviving such harsh living conditions. When we can't understand each other, it's far better to laugh about it than to get frustrated. Max, my host among the Sea Gypsies, said he was happy to now have a new son to help out. It is this kind of gentle jesting that tells me I am already accepted.

The importance of survival to the Sea Gypsies was evident from the get-go. There would be no long-winded discussions about what I wanted to do or how they felt about my presence. It was simply "get in the boat and let's go; we need to get food." So, after borrowing a net from a family member who lives in a stick hut, we took off to set the net and try for any food from the sea we could catch, including sharks, rays, and fish. But first up was a stop along the way with a crude handmade spear gun and sets of goggles to try our luck at spear-fishing. Almost immediately, Max caught a ray and I caught a puffer fish.

The Sea Gypsies are equally at home in the water and floating on top of it. They take to the water the way we would walk out in our backyard or go for a stroll down the street. Still, they don't really do it for enjoyment; that is to say, they don't swim just to swim or even to escape the heat. Their skin never feels the rinsing of a freshwater shower. They go in the salty ocean water to get food; the ocean is their grocery store. Still, it's a vast grocery store and they may need to travel miles to find what they want.

Max later explained to me through an interpreter that they have better fishing now than they have had in years. But the reason is a sinister one: the predators, sharks, are gone. You see, the Sea Gypsies are sometimes employed by Malaysian fishing boats to catch sharks for Asian markets; it's the fins they prize the most. These "fishermen" cut off the sharks' fins at sea, right after pulling them from their nets, while the animals are still alive. The body of the shark, still very much alive, is then dropped back into the water to writhe in an agonizing slow death. Max explained that he doesn't know where the sharks have gone, but he thinks they will return. (The Sea Bajau don't really think of the ocean as having a finite limit—to them, it goes on forever. I think differently, knowing that, in cleaning out the shark population, they have decimated the species, leaving little room for return.)

HAVING HAD THE CHANCE to spend time with many peoples in remote places, I've learned that they tend to eat only once a day. Living like that would scare the crap out of most of us in the civilized world, but on the ocean and in the deserts and jungles it isn't given a second thought. But then, I've noticed something else, too. Their days are not filled with stresses of modern living. They think about eating, getting water, fixing their hut, making a baby . . . and that's about it. So nervous energy doesn't burn away calories, and cultural conditioning does not make them claim they are "starving" after going four hours without food. Luckily, I too have lost all fear and panic of "starving" when I go a morning or even an entire day without food. Nor do I worry about my dog or kids starving after four hours without food. That said, the Sea Gypsies still rely on each other to get a full meal. While we were cleaning the fish we had just caught, a cousin pulled up in a boat to combine meals. He had the rice (which was traded for sea cucumbers at the local market) and we had the fresh fish. Dinner is served!

Another similarity I've observed among remote cultures is the concept of the meticulously clean living space. At first blush, most of these places look grotty from the outside. But once you live in it you realize that great attention is paid to spills and dropped bits of food. With such little space, everything has its place and must be returned to it. Many items need to be hung, for there are no shelves or cupboards here, no spare rooms or basements, no closets or attics. Everything is within hand's reach. So they can't afford to live like slobs in their tiny boats and huts, and they certainly can't become hoarders. Yet despite the cleanliness of boats, houses, shelters, and igloos around the world, one thing remains: the odor.

The stench of body sweat, cigarette smoke, old clothes, baby smells, and, in this case, the sea itself hangs heavy in the midday air under the stifling heat of an oppressive tropical sun. And all of it collects and remains under the plastic tarp only three-and-a-half feet high for four visiting kids (from the next boat over) and four adults. It's a good thing I had training during my youth to handle this kind of gathering, from years of visiting my rural relatives who chain-smoked and drank beer like it was an occupation.

One of the sad realities of my visit to the Sea Gypsies is that my presence may have made them more prone to attack from the many pirates in the area. Usually pirates pay no attention to the poor Sea Gypsies with their meager belongings; but add one white guy with camera equipment, and the potential for being kidnapped increases dramatically. Only a short while before I arrived, 20 dive tourists were kidnapped by pirates. One woman was shot and killed.

Here in the South China Sea, kidnapping has become a practice based on economics. The pirates often have no cause they believe in—they don't want any prisoners released or governments overthrown. Theirs is simply a matter of enterprise: kidnap a few tourists and release them for the cash. No greater incentive than that has built up an industry of piracy in different parts of the world. It's a potential problem I would have to face on a number of ocean crossings throughout my journeys. In my case, I'm not sure whether being a TV celebrity is a good thing or a bad thing. The local military wouldn't let me stay out on the Sea Gypsies' boat overnight without providing a nearby escort to watch over us. It lent an ominous overtone to the whole experience, especially since Max wanted to drop anchor out on the edge of the village facing the open ocean.

Back out on the ocean the next day with Max and his family, we went to check our nets, which yielded only two sea turtles—a beautiful and besieged reptile disappearing from the oceans at an alarming pace. Luckily I wouldn't have to bite my lip about the killing and eating of these wondrous creatures, since the Sea Bajau don't eat them. They respect the laws of protection that exist in this area, which is known as the turtle capital of the world.

A short while later we found ourselves on land to pick up some firewood. Suddenly I felt the effects of living in a boat. The land seemed like it was undulating and I wondered if, in fact, one of the reasons the Sea Bajau prefer life on the ocean is because they are simply unaware that this nauseating "land sick" feeling eventually goes away. Perhaps they figure it's just a reality of walking on land, and they want no part of it. Who wants to feel like throwing up all the time?

We climbed a short way into the jungle, gathering firewood and coconuts. Despite my nausea, I was relieved to finally stretch my legs on solid ground. Although I would have enjoyed another day with Max and his family, I had previously arranged to spend some time with those Sea Gypsies who prefer life in a stick hut to that in a small boat: the Gypsies who were the next step up the ladder; the *middle-class* Gypsies so to speak.

Sea Gypsy stick huts are perched above the water on a half-dozen spindly poles that are twisted down into the sandy bottom below. The water here is about only 10 feet deep, give or take the tidal flow. The homes are small, about 40 square feet, but still might house nine people and one cat. Sleeping quarters are tight, not to mention rustic. The bathroom is a hole in the middle of the hut, open to the water below. Fortunately I wasn't eating much so I didn't have to use facilities that were only feet away from all the inhabitants of the hut. The water below serves as sink, laundry tub, and bathroom all at the same time. So while one child is going poo in the hole, the woman of the hut is dropping a basket of clothing or sea cucumbers to be rinsed off a few feet away in the tropical ocean water.

The handful of little kids in this family are so accustomed to the dimensions of the hut—not to mention the numerous holes in its floor—they could actually run around and play a game of tag. They weren't perfect, though. More than once while I was there some little kid fell out of his family's hut, dropping six feet below into the calm ocean water. And then you would hear the inevitable crying.

There were so many stick huts grouped together here at the edge of the shore that it seemed much like a little stick-hut suburb: a hundred homes or more lined up in rows as if there were imaginary streets in the ocean waters below. These Sea Gypsies live a slightly more conventional lifestyle than the families on the boats, only in that they trade the fish and sea cucumbers they catch for clothes and other items at a nearby market. The boat-dwelling gypsies don't seem to involve themselves in the market much, if at all.

On this, my first morning, I was to join the ladies and head to the island for water from the one exist-ing well. They keep a few plastic jugs on hand for freshwater so that a trip to the land happens once every three days. All their cooking is done in the saltwater (most food is boiled), so the freshwater is reserved for drinking, a wise strategy under the intense tropical sun. The water from the island well is warm and salty. I drank it not knowing how many pathogens might be living in it.

We pushed the little boat off the shore after our water collection. The woman of the house where I was staying stepped onto the bow and squatted in a particular position—one that only the remote peoples of our planet seem able to manage. Not even my yoga friends are able to squat with the flats of both feet and their butts touching the ground at the same time. Yet people like the Sea Bajau come by this ability honestly, since it's a by-product of life without chairs. Sitting directly on the ground would make you filthy—not to mention vulnerable to bites and stings—and every remote culture I've met has this squatting ability.

Another skill that exists among tropical peoples is the ability to climb palm trees quickly and effi-ciently. They start as little kids when, like children everywhere, they're little monkeys without fear of heights or falling. But when coconuts play such an integral role in your life, you never lose the skill. The same goes for weaving the palm leaves they cut down while collecting coconuts. Weaving is done virtually the same way throughout the tropics by cultures thousands of miles apart from each other. Palm leaves are in great supply and offer perfect protection from tropical elements.

While gathering the palm fronds to repair their hut, the man of the house admitted that he would like to live on the land. But there's nowhere he's allowed to go. So in his case, life on the sea is forced: the Malaysian government does not recognize his people or even want to admit they exist. Sea Gypsies live, or float, between worlds.

The hut needed repair and some additional room, which prompted a great opportunity to take another trip to the island, this time to gather poles and palm fronds. Unfortunately there didn't seem to be a nearby "Hut Depot," so we worked in the jungle while watching out for poisonous snakes and stinging insects lurking in the wet foliage.

Once back at the hut, we got to work. First we pulled down all the old and dead palm fronds that made the walls of the hut itself. As we proceeded, hundreds of cockroaches fell out of the old palm fronds. The youngest member of the family, a 3-year-old, giggled with delight as she ran around killing them with a small stick. (It was like a scene from an Alfred Hitchcock movie!) The very friendly and talkative woman of the house climbed precariously above the waves from stilt to stilt to attach the fresh palm fronds to the outside of the hut. We then dove beneath the waves to stick long poles into the sand—these would support a platform for drying fish. Cross-poles were all laid down and tied on with leaves until the entire structure was fairly steady and secure.

In doing this work, I discovered that the waters here are not as benign as they look. Laura Bombier, my photographer and partner on this book, held her breath and dove down a few feet to photograph me working with the Sea Gypsies. Suddenly I heard her screams from under the water. She splashed to the surface still shouting, and I could see her trembling with pain. She had accidentally shoved her hand into a crown-of-thorns starfish (wrongly identified as a sea urchin in the TV series) that embedded dozens of painful little spikes into her hand. Her injuries weren't the only ones experienced by my crew during our year in the far-flung corners of the world: cameraman Peter Esteves has been stung by hornets; cameraman Johnny Askwith has been thrown from a horse; Andrew Sheppard and Dan Reynolds both got malaria; and virtually everyone has suffered from food poisoning. Funny, though—none of these things (other than the food issues) ever happens to me. Silly camera crew, they should watch what they're doing!

Not surprisingly, the Sea Gypsies knew exactly what to do to take care of Laura's stings. They peed in the water where it happened, which is said to appease the spirit of the sea. They wanted to pee on her hand, too, but she declined the treatment. I also offered. She declined again.

My last activity with the Sea Gypsies was to take part in compression diving for sea cucumbers. These creatures look like 18-inch-long sea slugs. As exotic as it sounds, compression diving is serious business. Every year, people die from doing it. The Sea Bajau used to free dive for sea cucumbers, which was dangerous enough. Now they have found a way to use their scavenged boat engines to push air down through a hose to the diver beneath the water.

If this all sounds a bit nasty, it is. They use vegetable oil for the engines, so the air you breathe tastes like rancid french-fry oil. It's disgusting and causes immediate heartburn. Imagine sticking your head right above a vat of hot cooking oil and inhaling deeply. But regular engine failures notwithstanding, they taught me the technique, handed me a hose, and sent me down with one of their divers.

It's an odd feeling at first, but relatively easy to get the hang of. Since you don't suck in the air like you do for scuba diving—the air is constantly being forced down the hose by the engine pressure—you simply bite down on the hose and let the oil-scented air flow into the mouth. You have to wrap the hose around your body so it doesn't rip out of your mouth on a piece of coral or something. But that still happened more than once, to no shortage of panic while I frantically tried to shove the flailing hose back between my teeth. It's like the reverse of the comical moment when a water hose flails around on the grass like a snake. Instead it is a hose blasting out bubbles and whipping around under the water while I try to catch it before I drown 45 feet down. You can stay down as long as you want, go as far as the hose will let you, and keep looking for bounty . . . so long as the rusty old engine doesn't quit on you. These Sea Gypsy divers push the limits because the Asian markets always want more sea cucumbers. They dive farther and deeper, and they expose themselves to great risk . . . just to survive.

After a week with the Bajau, I began to wonder when my time would come to experience some kind of ceremony. Since they focus on daily living in their hand-to-mouth existence, ceremony is not the first priority in their lives. They either have freshwater or need to get it. They either have some fish to eat or need to go catch some. So there's little time left for ceremony.

Still, they did have a ceremony: an offering to the sea to pay their respects and ensure safety and bounty. In their short and simple way, the Sea Gypsies express something they know inherently. *They are tied to the natural world for survival.* We are, too, though we don't act like it. So the Sea Bajau practice an exchange by offering rice or money, which they sink beneath the waves. Just as the natives of North America offer tobacco and the Incan people offer coca leaves, the Sea Gypsies make these humble offerings to Mother Earth herself. It is a matter of reciprocity. The earth gives to us, so we give back in honor.

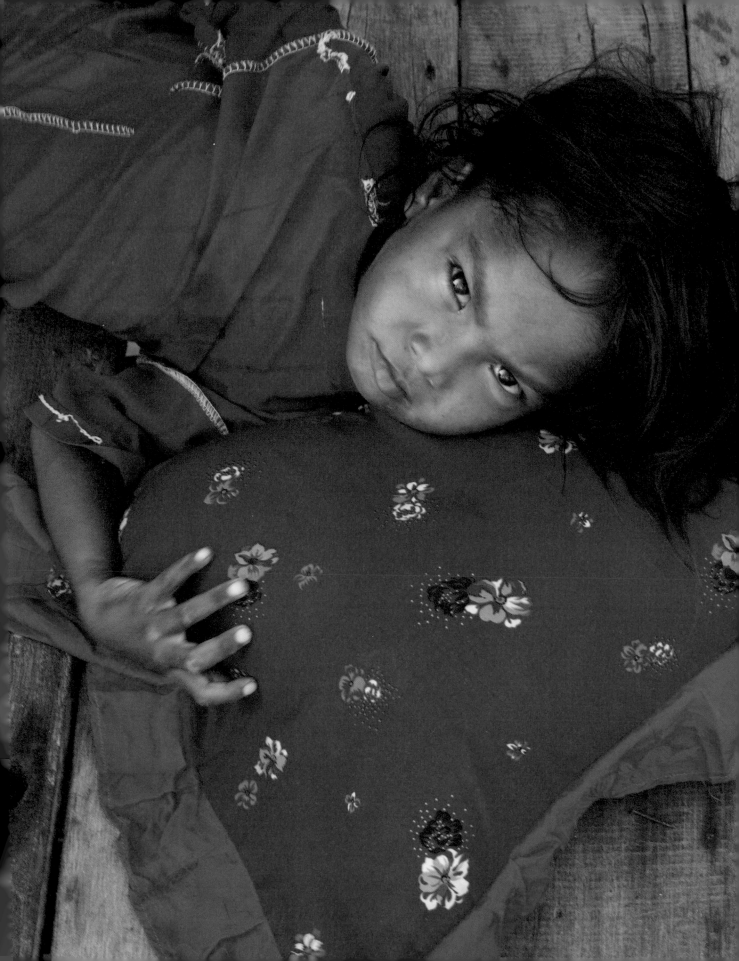

Until very recently, the Sea Bajau have had to survive only the forces of nature and the ways of the earth. But what faces them in the future is the encroachment of modern civilization and, perhaps more important, the consequences of humankind's destruction of the sea . . . their home. They are surrounded by a resource-hungry Malaysian society. They are scattered among islands that are only a short boat ride from massive international shipping ports and polluted Malaysian sea waters. I found the ports of this region to be the most disgusting I have ever seen.

The Sea Gypsies see it and are well aware of it. Yet they cling to their lifestyle and hope their children will also keep up this life. They don't know what is coming. I honestly can't see their lifestyle surviving much longer in this modern world. On the other hand, perhaps they will just keep island hopping until they run out of little coves to live in.

The Sea Bajau ceremony seemed so humble compared with the scarification and trance dancing I had already experienced. Yet it somehow affected me more profoundly. It was a subtle but powerful connection to the earth and its oceans, the very place that their survival—and my own—is impossible without. In respecting it, honoring it, and offering a humble exchange to ensure future survival, they recognize that there are bigger forces at work here.

Yet I was not to linger in this place of interconnectedness for too long. In massive contrast, my next journey would rip me from this subtle and respectful frame of spiritual belief and thrust me into a narcissistic, self-focused belief system that seems to exist to support only the individual's own personal circumstances.

Sea cucumbers are oblong, hairy, gelatinous creatures that live on the sea floor. They have one of the weirdest self-defense mechanisms on the planet: they expel their toxic digestive tracts when threatened and then quickly grow new ones. You have to slit open the belly and remove the guts. Chop up gutted sea cucumbers into bite-size chunks and fry them alongside anything that will give them some actual flavor. Sadly, they're being wiped out quickly in the Asian south seas and in areas such as the waters surrounding Fiji and Tonga. Boats from Thailand and other Asian nations pay fishermen a year's wages for a week's work to dive down and wipe out the sea cucumber population for their market. The sea cucumbers are vital to the health of the reef. Without them, the reefs die, as in the case of Tonga just a couple of years ago.

5

DANCING WITH THE DEVIL

The Singalese

If the Sea Gypsies' humble approach to ceremony lent a subtle yet profound atmosphere for my journey of the soul and adventures around the globe, then the devil dancers of Sri Lanka would swing the pendulum fully to the other side. Max and the other Sea Gypsies live simply, on and by the sea. They pay respect to its life-giving forces with a simple yet profoundly touching ceremony. Yet the dichotomy between the simple life of the Sea Gypsies and the island of Sri Lanka and the flashy, colorful, and perplexing lifestyle of the Singalese gave me cause for some personal head-shaking. It was like going from hangin' out with the Mormons in Utah to mingling with the Hollywood club scene . . . only weirder. Whereas the Sea Gypsies gently honor the waves that lap against their boats, the Sri Lankans perform exorcisms while wearing elaborate costumes and dancing with the devil.

My time on Sri Lanka started out in much the same way as previous shows we had shot with other cultures. It focused on the survival techniques of the Singalese (the people who call this part of Sri Lanka home), including the extraordinarily photogenic activity of stick fishing. I even jumped into a mud pit with an elder woman to dredge up soaking coconut husks, which the Singalese use to make rope and other things. As cool as I felt that looked on camera, it pales in comparison to stick fishing. It looks damn near impossible in photographs, yet stick fishing is an art that's not too tricky once you get the hang of it, provided your butt has a bit of fat for padding. My butt makes the cut.

Building the pole that will support a single man is easy enough—it's done on the land. The next stage, getting it to stick and hold in the sand at the bottom of the ocean, is another thing altogether. Two or three of us would swim out to a depth of about 10 feet of water and, with the ocean waves coming in, take turns free diving to the bottom and rocking the pole end back and forth to get it to sink deeper into the sandy ocean floor. Surprisingly, it didn't take long before the pole actually held. Two small poles tied to that large vertical one created a triangle just above the surface of the water, forming the perch onto which I would put my well-padded butt. The next challenge was climbing up the pole like a monkey out of the water and positioning my butt and legs just so. It looked ridiculously precarious but was in fact quite stable once I got over the fact that my butt would be perched on a skinny stick for many hours.

Wave after wave of small fish would make their way past the pole and, using a simple stick, some line, and a shiny bit of metal fishing lure, we would jig for them in the hopes of sticking a hook through their sides or in their mouths as they attacked the fake bait.

This part of the Sri Lankan coast was hit hard by the tsunami of 2004, and the results were devastating in many ways. As support poured in from the outside world, it was meted out to give priority to those with greater need. As a result, the rich—who had much but lost it all—became poor, while the poor—who had nothing and so were given much support—became rich. It was such a huge change that they called the tsunami the "Golden Wave." And the change happened nearly overnight.

While walking past boats strewn a quarter-mile inland, I learned from my Sri Lankan hosts about their rapidly fading culture and lifestyle. Where hundreds of stick fishermen once dotted the waters a few hundred yards from the land, only a dozen remained scattered here and there. In fact, thousands of fishermen were killed by the tsunami and, with their lives, went the culture of stick fishing . . . and devil dancing.

Why was devil dancing disappearing, and what was the connection to the fishermen themselves? As it is around the world, people who live on the sea tend to be highly superstitious and, therefore, keep many traditions alive. Devil dancing is a superstitious belief system held in high reverence by the most superstitious of the Singalese, their fishermen. Forty thousand people died in the tsunami, and most of the Sri Lankans were fishermen—the keepers of the spiritual traditions.

As Western aid poured in after the tsunami, distractions also entered traditional Sri Lanka in the form of the Internet, iPods playing Western music, and similar technology. The Golden Wave made it easy for the Lady Gagas and Britney Spearses of the world to distract the younger generation from adhering to the old, outdated, and freaky religious beliefs of their parents and grandparents. So, where a devil dance was once held nearly every night in multiple locations, it is now performed only once a month. Thankfully, my hosts were very happy to involve me in the exorcism process.

Few remote cultures are without their dogs, and the Singalese are no different. The canines I saw in Sri Lanka were by far the most pathetic looking I've ever seen, and that's saying a lot. Feral dogs are always mangy, flea-ridden, disgusting-looking, scrawny little things. But the ones in Sri Lanka were particularly gross. They really looked like they needed to be put out of their misery. They were, of course, afraid of humans, but had to hang around for survival. I imagine none of them has ever known the feeling of being snuggled.

The Singalese have a demon for *everything*: from your flu sniffle to the loud barking dog to the car accident you were in to various diseases to your financial circumstances to the amount of mosquitoes buzzing around your head. They believe the island is home to millions of demons, and their obsession with black magic has lasted for more than 2,500 years.

In fact, demon culture is so prevalent here that the Singalese believe an inland tribe, the Veddha (who lived in caves up until 1986), are half-demon/half-human and were spawned from demons. Not everyone has embraced the culture, however. During the period of colonial expansion and Christian proselytizing, the British first pushed the culture of demonism down to the southwest part of Sri Lanka. It was further sequestered to the coastline by encroaching Western culture. But it was the tsunami, which hit from the ocean side, that dealt a fatal blow to devil dancing. For six months after the catastrophe, not a single dance was performed, when once it was daily.

For the older Singalese, however, it's still the only way to improve your fortune. So, if you want to get better, be richer, exact vengeance, or clean up the mess in your yard, you need to be exorcised, which is the Singalese way of turning to the demons and trying to appease them so they stop whatever they're doing to make your life difficult. The only cure from demon possession is through a devil dance exorcism.

To perform an exorcism, you need a patient. And in this case, that patient was to be me! In fact the Singalese took it quite seriously, and I wasn't allowed just to *pretend* to be sick. They wanted to know something deep and dark—or at least something real—whose demon they could exorcise out of me. Luckily I had had many conversations with my local fixer, Jason Schoonover, months before I made this trip, so I had ample opportunity to select an affliction they could work on. Well, with so many to choose from, I wasn't sure what to offer them, and apparently exorcising an ex-wife is not part of the deal! I chose my fear of heights and the stresses of my career . . . and that is as deep and dark as I get.

The exorcism is an elaborate, through-the-night ritual. For me, that night's sacrifice would be a chicken, though in olden times it may very well have been a human. The dance is initiated by men dressed as women. The demons love vice, and women are seen to represent it. So what better way to entice the demons than to trick them into believing there are dancing women about?

Before the devil dance began, I had to spend a few hours with a priest by the ocean who cleansed and prepared me for the upcoming activities. I had to be dressed in white from head to toe. I struggled with the Catholic overtones, but the resemblance was only superficial. The priest burned incense and chanted over me to protect and prepare me for the exorcism, lest those nasty demons got an even greater hold of me. The timing of the ceremony was vitally important. Demons come out at specific times of the day, as well as all night long. So that I wouldn't be possessed during a critical step in the process, my cleansing had to take place outside those daylight times. It was tough on my ability to concentrate. Johnny Askwith, my camera operator, had set up his big jib arm to film everything, so the entire scene resembled a bizarre hybrid between a Christian mass and a Hollywood movie set. Perhaps it was an appropriate beginning to what I was yet to experience that night. My personal motives for being involved were not at risk, but my ability to really "buy into" the exorcism process was definitely taking a hit of skeptical reality.

Despite my preparations, I wasn't sure what to expect. The surroundings were decorated almost as if for a wedding. Throughout the day, people from the village tended to torches, plants, and overhanging decorations. I truly thought that, maybe this time, I would see or feel something extraordinary—perhaps an apparition. Was I about to mess with something dark enough to scare the crap out of me? These people took their exorcisms very seriously. They told me of strange voices and possession experiences that cause people to faint.

The high priest of the exorcism—the emcee, if you will—is called a Yakadura. He uses the combined energies of dancers, torch bearers, and the audience to assist in the exorcism. The dancers and drummers keep the action fast and lively all night long. The reasoning is simple. They and the Yakadura need the combined energy of the onlookers, who often number a hundred or more, to help with the exorcism. So the members of the audience must be kept awake. I glanced at Jason, who, after a long day of organizing, was already sleeping while sitting up. It wasn't working on him.

I sat at the edge of the circle with a pretty young Singalese woman who was there to act as my interpreter. We both wore white. They took the chicken and either broke its neck or hypnotized it with some muscle manipulation and smoke. Then they dragged the chicken (dead or alive, I couldn't tell) around my head and body. No blood was evident, and my guess was that the chicken represented a sacrifice for demons to show up (those nasty demons, demigods, and deities sure do require their sacrifices). Now things were about to get tedious. While my camera crew scuttled about for nearly 12 hours of exorcism activities through the dark of the night, enjoying the luxuries of coffee and conversation, I had to sit still and pay attention to the entire dance without a single break. If I didn't have any devils to start with, I certainly felt possessed—thanks to sheer exhaustion—by the time the night was over.

The Yakadura have a routine to follow regardless of your afflictions. They must entice out of you the six primary demons and 18 apparitions that cause disease. These demons are represented by Singalese men who emerge from behind a bamboo blind wearing costumes and masks: white masks to represent women of high caste; red masks for bloodthirsty demons; blue ones for aboriginal tribes, native gods, or deities; and black ones for the men of the moors.

To be honest, it all started to look very much like performance art . . . good performance art, but performance art nonetheless. So my psyche wasn't really feeling any effect of an exorcism. There were no ghosts in the smoke, faces in the flames of a torch, or anything like that. My skeptical side was holding strong this night.

Each individual demon (a person in a costume and mask) appeared and then spoke to the Yakadura while standing in front of me, agreeing that he (the demon) had caused some problems. The Yakadura asks, commands, or tricks the demon into leaving the body of the patient, freeing him or her from the affliction. "My" demon left and we waited through more dancing and drumming until another appeared. Then the drummers went silent again and let the demon and the Yakadura do their thing center stage. I cannot overstate the patience it took to sit there and listen to two costumed men talking to each other, as if onstage in a play, in a language I couldn't understand. The level of verbosity was mind-numbingly astounding. But the constant drumming between these talking sections had the greatest effect on me. It was hypnotic, the pulsating rhythm pumping through my body. But, mostly, I wanted to jam with them.

I sat through it all: the talented dancing of the men dressed in drag and holding lit torches; the long commentaries by the Yakadura that I could not understand; the arrival of various demons (often the same guy in a new costume) to converse with the priest. It was a test of patience to be sure. I got to recognize which man was behind which mask of which demon and to know whether the next scene was about to become highly entertaining or not.

It was a tediously long night that required me to sit motionless on that mat for hours on hours. The last part of the performance, taking place in the rising daylight sun, seemed the most meaningful as a priest-like man—who hadn't been very visible in this experience throughout the night—came and crushed lemon after lemon on my head. This was a final cleansing process. He took it very seriously, and so did I, even though I could tell my crew was going out of their minds from boredom. (In fact, they were already packing up.) But understanding my role in bridging the two worlds—the pragmatic (filmmaking) and the spiritual—was critical as I forced my crew to stay alert and reminded them that they had just spent a night filming history. No one had filmed such a devil dance before, at least not professionally.

It all felt very much like a carnival. At times it seemed like the dancers were gathering in the basement of a local hall to practice their dancing for an upcoming festival. I wondered where the tour bus was. I'm not suggesting that it felt faked. To the Singalese there was nothing fake about it. They took it very seriously. And I, just as I must always do when involved in such activities, took it very seriously, too. In my mind I wasn't there just to shoot a TV show; I was there to experience something profound and to see how it affected my life.

But my internal struggle continued. It was a culturally rich experience, but it *felt* like a show. The emotions and intent behind the scarification in South Africa moved some to tears and felt warm and meaningful, like a blessing. The metaphysics behind the trance dancing in the Kalahari seemed to have a basis in something potentially very real. The subtlety of the offering with the Sea Gypsies seemed utterly appropriate and humbled me. And now, here I was fighting boredom as my true personal demon—skepticism—was coming to the forefront of my mind. Maybe they really were exorcising my demons after all.

In light of the arbitrary scheduling of my various ceremonies it would seem that steps one and two (the scarification and trance dancing) seemed to be all about preparation and protection. Steps three and four (the Sea Gypsies and the devil dancing) seemed to be about learning how to process it all.

With the long night of exorcism behind me, we made our way inland to the city of Kandy, and the Queen's Hotel. I loved the hotel because it was rich in colonial history and because I got to see thousands of giant fruit bats blacken the sky each night around dusk as they took flight across the city. This was a welcomed conventional stopover on my way to visit the less modernized Veddha people, whom coastal people consider to be half-demon/half-human.

On our first night at the hotel, I made my way to the bathroom around 3 a.m. to take up my all-too-common position on the floor during trips like this one. I lay in the fetal position simultaneously throwing up and having diarrhea. The bowel pains were enough to bring me to tears. If I seem to be relating this in a nonchalant way, it's because it's such a regular occurrence for many people who travel the world and eat and drink things our Western bodies aren't used to. I'm used to it—the pain, that is—so when it happens I just get that "uh oh, here it comes again" feeling. Traveler's belly as it is nicknamed. These days I try to not eat or drink anything at all while traveling through developing countries like Malaysia. But living off power bars isn't fun, either. At least I was never alone; one of the crew was always suffering as well.

Visiting the Veddha deep inland on the island of Sri Lanka began on a perplexing note. When we pulled up to meet our hosts in the traditional village called Dambana, it seemed like a typical clichéd native village *museum,* complete with a giant tourism sign out on the road with a big arrow, black-and-white photographs in buildings, old utensils and axes mounted on walls, and crafts you could buy from the rag-wearing Veddha who just happened to be sitting out front waiting for you. One particularly old Veddha man just hung out and let you take his picture . . . for a price. Coming off of the carnival-like atmosphere of the Singalese devil dancing I was not in a good mood to begin with.

It was my worst nightmare, a human petting zoo. I've been to similar places all over. They run the gamut from native-operated centers where the guy doing the leather-making and fire-starting demonstrations wears an Eminem T-shirt and can't wait to get home to his favorite TV show (usually *Survivorman,* thank you) to beautiful, elaborate dances and powwows presented with great heart and meaning. Here I now was with the last vestige of an aboriginal people, the Veddha, living in a little museum in Sri Lanka.

As for the Veddha, I couldn't tell how they perceived it all. They looked the part, but you could see a few of them being driven away in a bus to go to their "real" homes. I saw the occasional kid ride off on his bike, ghetto blaster held to his head. Before this first day was to be finished, it would only get worse.

I make my living as a filmmaker and musician, but I never compromise content just to make a show. I thrive on authenticity. So my next step was to walk behind the museum to the chief's house to ask permission to enter his village. It's important to note that it was *behind* the museum, because most tourists aren't allowed to share this experience. As always, though, I was pushing the boundaries to get to the real Veddha. They have a few hundred acres of land to farm and live on—supposedly *in their traditional way.* They have banned cell phones and TVs in an attempt to keep their culture alive. Everything *looked* appropriate, even the little house built out of mud and cow manure. We met, and they fed us a traditional feast that I enjoyed watching my crew choke back. To this day I don't know what was on our plates. Every chance I get, I make my *Beyond Survival* crew eat the disgusting things I have to eat. I never had that opportunity while filming *Survivorman* as I didn't have a crew with me for those shows. So now I don't let them get away with snickering behind the camera lens. I've seen more than one crew member vomit. It's my only way of getting back at them while they watch me do the things I have to do.

Something was missing here in the village. Where were the women? As it turns out, they were not allowed to come outside, not allowed to be seen. If the Singalese had a male-dominated lifestyle, then the Veddha took it to the extreme. The women's primary function, other than the obvious, is to cook the food after spending all day mixing wet cow dung and plastering the buildings with it. They're considered second-class citizens by the Veddha men.

The chief seemed arrogant and hesitated to work with us. When I run into this kind of attitude, it's panic time for me. Recognizing that my approach might have to be a little different here, I played to the chief's ego. In the end all was cool and I was given permission to carry on and try surviving with members of the Veddha community, who still live mostly on the land.

As I had before with many other cultures, I wanted to experience their lifestyle as they lived it *without* tourists present. It was going to take some communication to get them to understand this need, even though I had already explained it to the chief. These men actually *looked* prehistoric. Old and wrinkled, one or two of them were raised in caves.

In my first foray with the Veddha, they showed me how to set up different types of traps to catch wild game. This experience was great until I watched them knock down the traps before walking on. I asked them why. They explained they were just showing me. At this point I put on the brakes and pulled everyone together to set the rules straight. As always, I wanted no make-believe. The men were to live and survive as they would if I weren't here. No show and tell. If they don't use these traps now, then they shouldn't even bother showing them to me. They got it, and we had an understanding. And, as I might have guessed, these men of the jungle smiled with appreciation. They no more wanted to put on a show for me than when they do it at the museum. We finally found a place to bond and headed into the jungle to do our thing.

One of those "things" was the constant chewing of betel nut. This disgusting activity takes place throughout much of the Asian tropical world, including here in Sri Lanka. It's a complicated process. First the nut is broken up so that it can be put in the corner of the mouth. It's horribly bitter. Lye is then added to the mouth to mix with the betel nut, along with leaves and saliva, and to pull the chemicals out of the ingredients. This bitter mouth chew is bad enough, but then the Veddha add moldy and wet tobacco leaves to the mix. If you feel nauseated reading this recipe, imagine how I felt chewing this concoction. On occasion—depending on how much you chew—it gives you a high similar to a mild marijuana. Mostly, though, your face just becomes numb. The blood-colored spit you have to eject constantly from your mouth is why it became banned in cities in New Guinea. The streets were red with the dried spit.

The most exciting survival activity I was to do with the Veddha was poison fishing. I had read about poison fishing in magazines and seen it in films. Now I wanted to see if it works. We spent the better part of the morning walking a few miles in every direction in search of some particular tree or root or plant. At one location I found myself chopping into a tree with white sap splashing back at my face. At this point my companions decided to tell me that the sap was highly toxic and one drop in my eye could blind me. To emphasize their point, when I was done they hovered over me and removed every dab of tree sap they could find on my hands and clothing. Later we dug down into the ground beside a tree to expose the roots and chop them out for the concoction.

We had leaves to find as well. It never ceases to amaze me that, over the years, so many tribes around the world somehow figured out that just such combinations work perfectly together to create a lethal dose of poison. It's mind-boggling to then use this poison, without any prior knowledge of its components, to kill fish swimming in streams.

Once we had gathered everything, we walked through the Sri Lankan jungle to a spot where a stream widened slightly. We spent an hour or more blocking off the downstream flow with mud and grass to essentially create a 40-by-40-foot pool. The next step was to mash together all the ingredients in a canvas bag. Then, bag in hand, two other men and I jumped into the stream and swished the bag around so the poison would spread throughout the pool—while we were still in the water! My eyes widened as one by one fish simply floated to the surface, ready to be picked up by two of us wading in the stream. The Veddha couldn't explain what was happening. My guess is that the chemicals combined to either sting the fish or choke them out by depleting all the oxygen. But then, that's just my guess.

During all this poison fishing, the Veddha opened up to me. They complained about losing their homeland and being forced to live in this one small section of jungle. Without saying the actual words, they hinted about living in a human petting zoo. We walked for hours in the jungle, pulled honey out of beehives without using smoke, gathered ingredients, and poisoned more fish for a meal on the spot. The men showed me how to craft a bow slingshot. And it brought them joy. No other tourist had shown such interest. Indeed, when we had first arrived, a tour bus with a Japanese TV crew stopped at the museum and shot a bunch of scenes, I assume for a documentary about the Veddha. It was pathetic.

Yet back out in the jungle we were in our element. I trudged along in my big boots, the Veddha in their bare feet. Walking among the old men was a boy I thought to be about 18 years old who wore, well, almost nothing. We nicknamed him Mowgli (sorry, couldn't help it; he really looked just like the *Jungle Book* character), and he was the strongest and most eager in the group. He restored my confidence in what these men were all about because, although he was young, he was into it. I can tell you that the skills that all these men showed in the jungle were far beyond simply being part of their "show." They had to live this way for real to be able to pull it off. On the last night they performed their own version of the devil dance, and my compassion for them deepened.

This time, the dance was much darker and more intense, and we got a surprise. The Veddha used the trance dance in a way similar to the San of the Kalahari: they attempted to part the veil to the other world to gain key survival information from the spirits. This night they definitely got some information. We all met in the middle of the jungle at a clearing where they usually performed the dance for tourists. We had been camping in the heart of dangerous elephant territory the night before. I now felt comfortable with these men and their abilities and welcomed the return to camp and the reunion with my crew for this final devil dance.

There was no fanfare—just one tripod platform for offerings and a big fire. They have no need for masks, costumes, or decorations; they dance for guidance. They began their dancing as I sat close. They came over to me and dragged branches around me, chanted to me, and threw cleansing coconut water on me. Once again, it was all about protection and exorcism. They stepped on the fire with their bare feet. The drums kept the pulsating beat in the dark. Then something strange happened.

They became aware of my crew members, who were watching and filming the ceremony, and pulled one of them into the dance area where I sat. Normally the crew is forbidden to get involved, since even on a practical level it would ruin the footage for the TV series. So I was shocked when I saw Eric (not his real name) right in the middle, doing things even I wasn't asked to do.

The other crew members got upset and tried to motion for Eric to get out of there. One of our cameramen, Peter, was particularly pissed. But something was wrong. Eric was dancing away and stomping his feet just like the Veddha, only with a silly grin on his face. I, on the other hand, sat on the ground looking at Peter with a "WTF?" expression. Then it happened. Eric went as rigid as a board. One second, he was trembling and shaking violently while dancing and bouncing about; the next, he was straight as a piece of wood before our eyes. The Veddha seemed to expect this reaction and danced around him, shaking branches over him. They lowered him into their arms and carried him, still straight as a board but now with his eyes closed, over to a bench. They made some kind of quick motion on him while he lay on the flat bench, and he jolted upright. He was sitting up, eyes wide open, and smiling. He said he didn't remember anything, only that they yanked on his hair when they first pulled him into the fire dance.

Eric's exorcism came as no surprise to the Veddha, who told me that, from the day we arrived, they saw he was possessed and would need to be exorcised. They said the "entity" was following him around. Apparently they did their job well that evening. What they probably didn't know was that this week was the anniversary of his father's death, and that he'd confided to me earlier that he was feeling his dad's presence. He was even brought to tears—the first time in many years that he had cried over his loss.

Eric took great exception when I told him what the Veddha said about a demon following him around; he became angry with me because I think he felt we were equating the demon with his father's spiritual presence. But he had missed the point. The Veddha don't view demons in the traditional Hollywood sense, as you or I might—all dark and evil and scary. They simply believe in millions of "afterlife" entities. "Demon" is nothing more than a word they use to give these spirits a name. Eric's father was not a *demon* in the classic sense of the word; he was simply in his spiritual form and was in Eric's life at that point in time. The Veddha apparently saw this presence and wanted to set the spirit free. I don't think Eric has ever forgiven me for what I think was his misunderstanding over the Veddha's perspective. What is most freaky is that they picked up on it at all.

As our activities came to an end that night, the Veddha warned us to leave the area together and quickly, because the dance had attracted the attention of many demons. Not really paying attention to that warning, I made my last commentary to my camera completely alone in the dark and in the jungle. Everything was fine until a cold chill in the hot jungle night ripped up my spine. With that "creepy" feeling of being followed, I made tracks quickly. I suppose if I have a disappointment over this dance it is that Eric was affected and not me.

Once again I felt like the ultimate skeptic, sitting there and not feeling a thing.

GRAVE DIGGING
The Hewa

At the end of my first Survivorman episode in Papua New Guinea in 2009, one of the Hewa men (the local indigenous people) took Laura and me to see the above-ground grave of his brother, who had died of malaria. It was the first time I had ever seen a human skeleton. Surprisingly, it wasn't creepy at all. Here in the mountainous jungle, it seemed normal, even appropriate.

It was during this trip that my anthropological guide and interpreter, Bill Thomas, talked about a hidden secret ceremony called the Cumoutin. Roughly translated, it means a "coming out." The Hewa often bury their dead in a sitting position, with the top of the skull only inches under the surface of the earth. A few years later they return to the graves and exhume the bones. In some cases, they remove the skull just by "popping" it off and carrying it home. The bones are often placed on a specially decorated platform, where the soul is finally set free. The Hewa feel that, without this ceremony, the soul is never truly free. It is a tradition to display the skulls on decorated platforms, which is why early explorers thought the Hewa were cannibals.

Lutheran missionaries have forbidden this "heathen" practice for the past 40 years. The Hewa have continued, though always under the cover of secrecy. This is why nobody has ever seen such a ceremony, let alone filmed or photographed it. Even Bill, who had been coming here for 20 years, had never seen it. It was this particular ceremony that sparked the idea for *Beyond Survival with Les Stroud*, the TV series. I hoped I could film, and maybe even take part in, a ceremony that, even now, was forbidden and kept secret from outsiders. So two years after my first visit to Papua New Guinea and the Hewa people, I returned.

My first attempt at seeing a Cumoutin ceremony started out fantastically. The family from the village was keen. They had decorated themselves and invited me to decorate the platform that was to house the bones. We made offerings in preparation of unearthing the body. My crew and I were tense; we weren't sure what it was going to look like. For goodness' sake, I was about to become a grave robber (sort of).

But the climax I had hoped for was not to be. Before we began digging, a large group of people showed up, machetes in hand. An argument followed. Bill tried to interpret. His unsettled look told me it was bad news. Bill is big and muscular, and the Hewa respect and probably fear him. So if he was feeling nervous, my crew and I surely had something to worry about. It turned out that the people who showed up were from the mother's side of the dead man's family and had not been consulted about digging up the grave. Their machetes waving in the air, they were clearly not happy and refused to let us continue. The other Hewa apologized to us, but the day was done.

We decided to leave the village and make our way up the mountain to be with another family who also wanted to perform a Cumoutin. They were relatives of the Hewa below but preferred to live higher up, where the air is a little cooler. It would be a heck of a trek straight up and through the dense jungle foliage. Before we would make that trip, I focused on the usual survival traditions of the Hewa, as the TV series filming dictated: hunting with a dog, bow-and-arrow hunting, gathering, and raft building. All along, we moved ever farther up the mountain, closer to the second family willing to perform a Cumoutin.

Halfway up the mountain we came on a small family village and spent the night in a fairly large three-room, thatched-roof hut. The five or six men slept on one side while the women and children slept on the other. These protocols keep things straight for everyone, so emotions like jealousy remain in check. A fire on either side of the hut kept some cau cau—a potato-like plant—cooking for all of us to munch on.

The night was a strange and long one as I slept on the floor right in the middle of the hut. It was punctuated by constant tortured coughs and agonizing hacking from the babies, kids, and adults alike, the effect of the malaria they all have. Sometimes the babies' cries were normal, but other times you could tell they were moans of pain and suffering. Their skin was a mass of boils, scabs, dry flakes, and pus. Life expectancy here is 32 years.

To simplify our logistics, I took only three camera operators with me—Laura Bombier, Andrew Sheppard and Johnny Askwith—for this jungle hike. Both are tough and able-bodied guys, but Johnny has picked up a few extra pounds over the past few years, and the hikes were intense. Luckily he lightened the mood for all of us with his constant stream of expletives. "Oh, my God! Oh, my . . . I'm gonna die . . . we're all gonna die . . . motherfuck . . . oww . . . I'm gonna die . . . this is insane . . . insane . . . oww . . . mutha fuh"—as he slid in the mud behind me down into one valley, only to look straight up again at the next few hundred yards of mountain climbing up the other side. On one occasion we all stumbled upon a nest of large stinging, biting ants that covered an area of about two hundred square feet. Exhausted from many hours of jungle climbing we still found the energy to bolt like Olympic sprinters, while carrying heavy camera gear and swatting at ants landing on our heads from the trees above.

When we finally made it to the little hut high up on the mountain, the family was ready for us. They had completely decorated themselves, and the platform for the bones was ready. And so we began.

Handling corpses is a tricky process, and one in which you really shouldn't use your hands for fear of some pretty deadly diseases (such as meningitis or kuru). Immediately after we dug into the earth, the spiders, beetles, and scorpions appeared. But mostly there were ants. And they bit. They crawled over our feet and hands as we removed the earth. The sensation lent an ominous, creepy air to the whole experience.

We were delicate in our gestures, being careful not to dig too deep for fear of breaking or crushing the bones. At first some clothing appeared and we used tongs to lift individual pieces of bone out of the hole. At one point we lifted up a pant leg, and with it the entire leg bone.

But for the Hewa it wasn't creepy. It was reverent and respectful. This was our host's father. Tears were in every eye as more and more bones became visible. It was as if the person had just died. Emotions were strong and out in the open. A half-dozen or more men pitched in and took turns with the shovel. The Hewa had decorated themselves with armbands and headbands, which were attached to their bodies with beaded straps. It was their version of Sunday best. What was significant today was that not only was it the first time an outsider had seen such a thing, it was new to their kids, too. It was a statement of the Hewa reclaiming their spiritual traditions.

Eventually the moment came when the skull became accessible and this particular body was buried not upright but lying down flat. It was a moving and quiet moment. They gave the honor to me of lifting the skull out of the grave, and four of us held the shovel as we put it on the platform. It was a primitive ceremony in a very primitive place. It lacked the sophistication of a Sri Lankan devil dance. It lacked the metaphysical nature of the San Bushmen's trance dancing. But the main ingredient here was emotion.

The ceremony ended as we burned bananas over a smoky fire, a symbol of offering the dead man food for his journey. And then it was over. The spirit would take care of itself.

We made the long trek down to the village where they performed a sing-sing for me. Much like a North American powwow, the sing-sing is a chance for people to wear decorative clothing and headdresses and sing and dance to stories about hunting and life in the jungle. Though it was ultimately a lackluster event, I took part just the same, with all the integrity I could muster. Nothing could be taken away from the knowledge that I had just participated in, filmed, and photographed something never before seen by an outsider. Additionally, the younger generation had experienced some of their own culture. Perhaps they would someday keep the tradition alive.

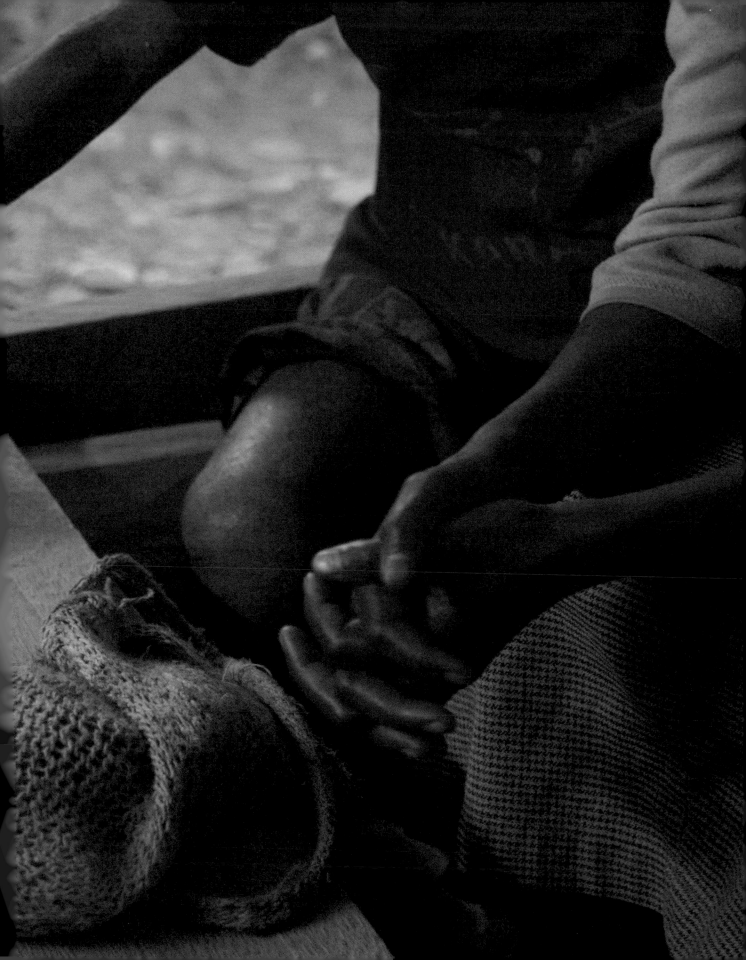

7

BLACK MAGIC AND THE SEED CEREMONY

The Antandroy

Until now, my experiences were only building blocks on my greater journey toward self-discovery, even though I didn't know it at the time. I had started out on a spiritual voyage of discovery, and each new adventure opened my eyes further. Some of the ceremonies seemed spiritual and metaphysical and might even hold more meaning than the experiences themselves conveyed. Others seemed like little more than cultural events, no matter how interesting and historic they were.

Seeking out remote peoples means calling on every resource and contact I can find. It was Johnny Askwith, my cameraman, who suggested Madagascar as a potential location for finding remote groups of people still living close to the land. As far as my personal journey was playing out, it seemed appropriate that the middle section of my year filming for the series was all about process: just show up, involve myself, and see what happens. Of all the experiences and ceremonies so far, the devil dancing in Sri Lanka had the outside appearance of being something very dark. But those dancers were about to be outdone by what seemed dangerously close to voodoo within the cultures of Madagascar, the world's fourth-largest island.

I spent time with two tribes while in Madagascar: the Antandroy, who live on the remote southern coastline; and the Antanosy, who live in the even more remote interior. With the Antandroy, my observations were limited to survival methods. They seemed to have no ceremony to speak of but loved to sing and dance. The ceremonial aspects of my visit to Madagascar and my journey into the world of the Antanosy would have to wait.

A major exporter of vanilla, Madagascar is not as remote as our Western perception would have us believe and looks nothing like the animated movie of the same name. Existing independently off the southeast coast of Africa in the Indian Ocean, the island seems prone to abuse from outside forces. For instance, it was here that I began to see how the long reach of Japan affects remote cultures. The Japanese had built roads in Madagascar as part of securing its ability to fish these waters, only to up and leave them without providing any maintenance. Now the country's roads are studded with car-eating potholes.

The Japanese did not, however, need to go to such lengths with Madagascar's coastal dwellers. These fishermen paddle simple dugout canoes and are not in any position to stop anyone from using their waters. Not surprisingly, the ocean bounty the Antandroy once enjoyed has been devastated by over-fishing, so these modest people have to travel farther every year to get a good catch.

The Antandroy are probably the handsomest people I have ever come across. The men are built like lightweight prizefighters; the women are striking. As a group, they stand in stark contrast to the rough-looking Hewa of Papua New Guinea. The Antandroy are also a very friendly people. They accepted me with big smiles and a caring attitude when I first entered their oceanside village—a scattering of tiny stick huts dotted along the sandy coastline.

Like so many remote peoples, they live in small twig huts where everyone sleeps almost on top of everyone else. A day does not go by that they aren't covered in sand in some way. Shoes are unknown. And like everywhere else in the world, the ocean provides plenty of garbage to be made into nets and other items.

The Japanese also built the only freshwater wells in the region, essentially forcing the Antandroy to congregate their little huts close to the freshwater. This is where they bring their cattle and fill their plastic buckets before starting the hike home, which could be just as close as around the next sand dune or as far as a few miles away.

The Antandroy live between two worlds. Their ocean supplies are dwindling, and, now that big industry has clear-cut the baobab forest, their farmland is turning to sand. The younger men leave the village and go work for the sisal industry, which has replaced logging as a primary source of income here. (Sisal is a plant that makes cordage.) That work—as well as influence from the outside world—continues to erode the culture of these coastal people. It's a simple existence jammed between a desert and the ocean. Salt and sand are constant companions in this life.

I loved my time surviving with the Antandroy. As part of that process, I had the distinct pleasure of partaking in one of their favorite pastimes: wrestling. Out on the sand people gather in a circle for a wrestling competition called ringa. In ringa, a combatant, when ready to wrestle, wears a scarf on his waist. He picks an opponent by handing him another scarf, and taunts him with joking dance moves and gestures. It was just my luck that the leader of the group, who happened to be the biggest and strongest-looking man, wanted to take me on. My competitive spirit rose to the occasion, and I threw him to the ground two matches in a row. The enjoyment and approval were evident in his and everyone else's laughter and cheering. To celebrate we went to a night of dance, song, and fishing out on the coral, under a torch-lit sky. The locals were quick to include me as family, an acceptance that will follow me throughout all my journeys yet to come.

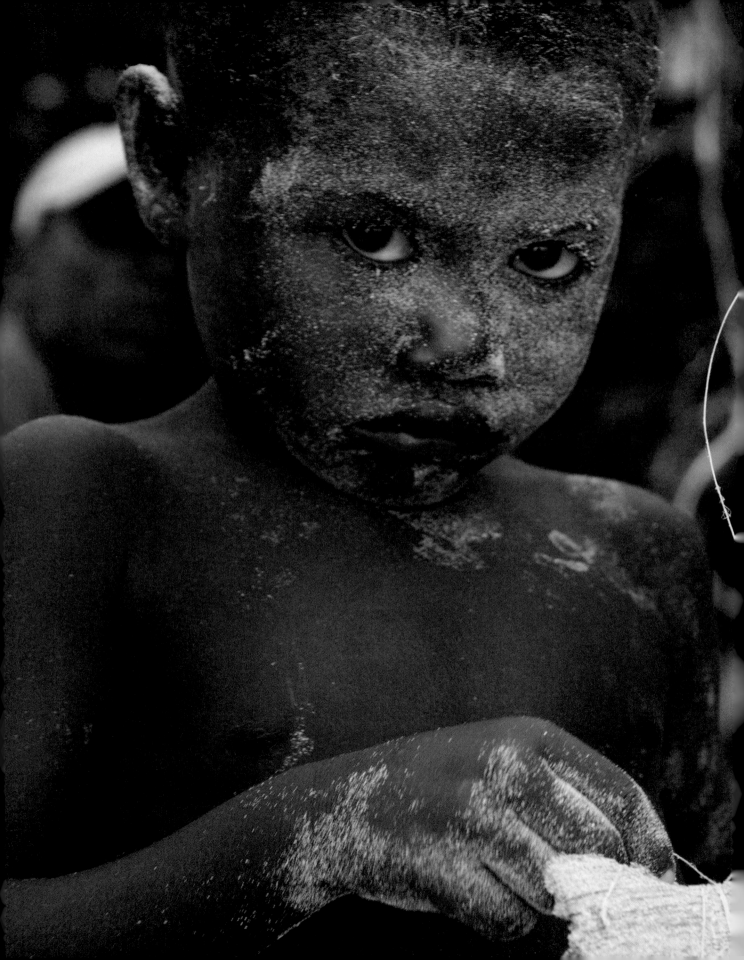

The real journey awaited me. Farther inland, the Antanosy tribe was known for a secret ceremony called a seed reading ceremony, an undertaking my research revealed to be an integral part of the culture of their lives. It's hard to know its origin, for, as I would learn, it was a strange hybrid of beliefs.

The Antanosy live a much simpler life than their coastal relatives to the south. It's not quite jungle here, but it's close. From the capital we drove many grueling hours over pothole-rutted roads to reach the interior of the country where they live. Their huts are tiny, dirty, and dark, and it struck me that it's one of the few places where people from a remote culture aren't meticulously clean . . . quite the opposite, actually.

Unfortunately we were not a self-contained filming unit and had to rely on Antanosy hospitality for sleeping and living quarters. It was great for the story of my journey, but it made life difficult for the crew. On the first night we were there, Laura, my son Logan, and another four crew members crowded into a tiny hut on a floor covered with rooster crap. We jerry-rigged our mosquito nets and hoped that the hand-sized spiders on the ceiling and the finger-length wasps flying around wouldn't bother us. It was a double-room hut, and a baby in the other room screamed all night long; no one would stop the howling. We were new guests, so we couldn't say anything. But between the spiders, the hourly rooster crowing, the crap-covered floor, and the baby, nobody slept that night. I was in a ripe mood for my next ceremony: the ancient seed reading ceremony.

There are plant-medicine ceremonies, in which the concoction is prepared and ready (often in a plastic bottle). Then there are ceremonies where you must first go out on to the land and gather all the necessary ingredients. The belief is that the particular plant is calling out to you. You pick and choose from among the roots, leaves, and vines just the right piece that speaks to you and connects with your soul and inner psyche. In a metaphysical way, I greatly prefer this method. It feels much more like you're having a pure, organic experience—as if you are connecting with the earth and its energies in a profound way, right from the beginning. Although groggy from the lack of sleep, I was pleased to travel throughout the small valley where the Antanosy live to gather just the right ingredients needed for the plant medicine. I believe success in these undertakings depends on your intentions. So if I'm the one to pick the leaves or dig up the roots and scrape the bark, then my good intentions are with all the energies right from the get-go.

The main purpose of this particular ceremony was to read my future and protect me for my journeying. The goal was to put me in a trance for visioning. The traditional healer, or shaman, is called a Mpisikidy. He has the gift of reading the seeds, a gift that's believed to be passed down from generation to generation. Like the San Bushmen of the Kalahari and the Sangoma in Africa, the Antanosy use their ceremony to communicate with the ancients so they can gather information about planting crops, hunting, and marrying. Individual decisions are made after the healer consults the ancients.

The seeds were laid out in various patterns from north to south to represent aspects of a person's life, and the shaman must interpret the message. Yet it's not always a positive experience. Opening a portal to the spirit world can be dangerous since not all spirits are benevolent, so great care must be taken lest you invite the wrong spirits to the party. For my protection, incense was burned and I was given liquids to consume.

Outside two women shamans were dressed in white. One was old and looked as if she had done thousands of these ceremonies. Her hair was beaded with dreadlocks, and she swung her neck back and forth. Her closed eyes pointed to the sky. Then she walked without once looking down. The other woman, who was shockingly young, truly looked "gone"—her eyes rolled back in their sockets as she tranced. The women, whose trances were underway when they entered the little hut where the male shaman and I were now busy reading the seeds, never smiled.

Small guitar-like instruments strummed relentlessly on the same dissonant chord; it seemed almost impossible that the young boys playing them could go on for so long. The shaman and I, sitting in the hut in the midday heat, continued going over the seeds. We drank plant medicine, and I listened to him chant. The women shamans, already in a state of trance, entered the hut and sat down. It was an intense cacophony of sound. We were now crammed with onlookers: elders supporting the process by watching intently and being a part of the general energy of the room; kids staring through slat holes in the walls. It was stifling hot, with the stench strong from bodies that have never seen a bar of soap. The chanting and percussion would not stop for hours, unless participants felt the need to stop and drink pure cane alcohol or smoke tobacco. Dressed all in white, I drank, too, as liquid was poured over my head. The women convulsed for hours in their seated positions as they helped invoke the trance-like state needed to communicate with the spirit world.

Many more hours passed. I felt nothing—only boredom. And then it happened. Everything seemed to become intense: the drumming, the heat, the drink, the chanting, the music, the smoke. The women shamans were now at a feverish state. For a moment, I could hear what was going on around me, but I didn't care. My own state of childlike fever made it all seem so distant. For the first time, my focus on what the cameramen were doing didn't matter. They called out my name. I could hear them, but I just didn't care to answer. I was getting close. I had come this far, and I didn't want to be pulled back. If they got it on film, they got it. If they didn't, they didn't. I didn't care. I didn't trance with the San Bushmen. I didn't get any messages with the Sangoma in South Africa. If this was my time to process everything, I wanted it now. I wanted to trance.

I felt like I was floating above myself, outside of the physical realm. But I didn't hear anything from another world; I saw no visions. I just felt satiated, numb. For the first time, I felt as though the film-making be damned. Maybe it was just the cane alcohol. Ultimately, it was only a moment. But it was my moment and I was going with it. For the first time, I was able to see in both directions at once: the spiritual side of enlightenment and the practical side of filmmaking. And the spiritual side was winning over my powers of concentration for the first time.

Was it voodoo or the cane alcohol (I didn't drink much of it)? Was it the plant medicines or the chanting? I'm not sure. It wasn't an overly profound moment, but I had had a glimpse into possibilities. The connection between the chanting, the music, the rattles, the "medicine," and my focus seemed to nudge me closer to some kind of insight. At the very least, it showed me that I could have powers of concentration stronger than my desire to double-check camera angles.

Returning to clear consciousness of my surroundings was much quicker than leaving it. I opened my eyes and reconnected with the film crew. In the sweaty heat of the Madagascar day we ate a disgusting-looking meal of slaughtered duck and who knows what else—it's best not to ask what was on the plate. If I was frustrated by one thing, it was that I never got any information from the shaman himself—no deep messages to pull out of the seed reading he did, no revelations to dwell on.

I left Madagascar feeling a little out of sorts from the episode, and I liked that feeling. I liked being a little knocked off my extremely rational and skeptical platform and pushed a little deeper into the realm of the unknown.

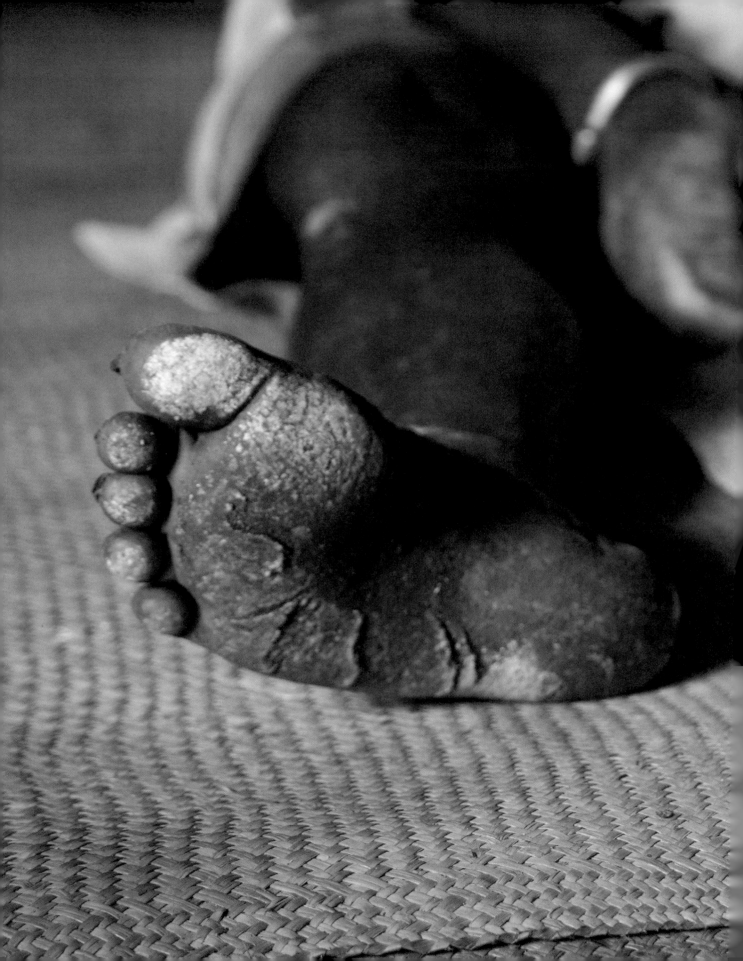

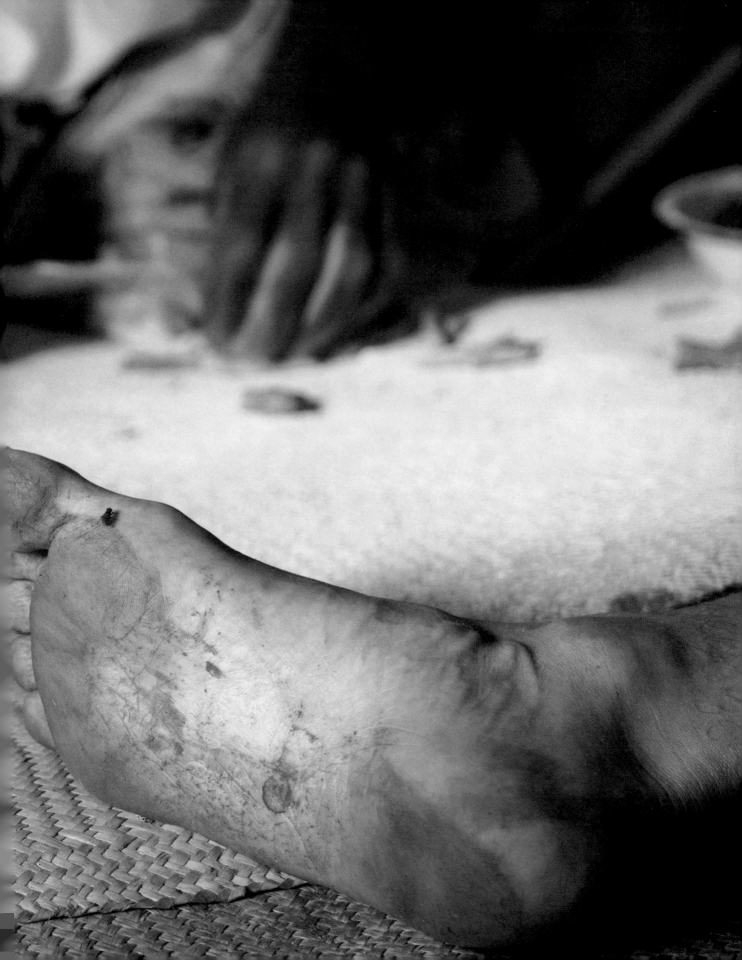

8

LIVING ON THE LAND

The Inuit

My head was still fuzzy from the seed ceremony in Madagascar as I boarded a plane for the Canadian High Arctic. I wasn't sure what I had experienced in that remote island on the other side of the world. Was it spiritual? Was it some kind of voodoo? Was it simply the result of the medicine I ingested in the tropical heat of the day? Or was it part of the process that I needed to go through to gain some deeper spiritual insight?

Until now, my experiences were in faraway and exotic places. But coming to Pond Inlet on Baffin Island felt like returning home. Not only was this Canada, but I had shot a *Survivorman* episode here. So I knew what to expect from both the people and the topography. I knew this land well and loved it very much. Anyone who visits the Arctic will tell you that you're never the same afterward; the land always seems to beckon you back. There is something in the vast barrenness and beauty that conspires to hold on to a piece of your soul so that when you finally do return, you feel like you're home.

But there was also what I perceived to be a problem: there were no ceremonial aspects to this trip. Our preproduction research uncovered nothing about Inuit shamans communicating with other worlds. Nobody was able to shape-shift into animals any more or speak to the ancients. It certainly was a rich part of Inuit history, but it was gone, long-ago gone. With the assimilation of the Inuit culture, the residential schools (church-run boarding schools, closed in the 1990s), and the movement into government-made townsites, the Inuit had lost one of the three sides of their cultural triangle: their sense of spirituality.

Although I knew there would be little or no ceremonial aspect to this adventure, I went out on the land with my Inuit guides feeling empathy toward their way of life and open to any experience. By the end of the week it became apparent that, although they may travel by modern snowmobile, use high-powered rifles, receive lots of government funding, and live in houses with all the modern conveniences you could imagine, the Inuit still seem to have a real connection to the land. All that they are about, and all that they do, still focuses on getting out for a hunt, eating caribou and seal, and maintaining land-based skills for survival should they be stuck, alone and a long way from help (which happens often).

Survival here requires a deep knowledge of the land and an intimacy with it. And the Inuit have not lost that intimacy. To this day it remains a by-product skill set of living in a remote region of the planet. Planes and ships may have brought the outside world here, but not yet to the point where the old ways can be forgotten and left to legend and history books. You may be able to find incredibly expensive milk and a very old bucket of Kentucky Fried Chicken in the grocery store freezer ($50.00 for the KFC), but there is still a stronger desire to eat "grocery" items obtained from hunting on the land.

To be sure, there is no shortage of drinking booze and sitting around watching TV, especially in the six months of winter darkness (ironically, *Survivorman* and *Beyond Survival* are very popular up here, too). But for most residents, the flow of the year still revolves around the caribou hunt, the seal hunt, the narwhal hunt, or arctic char fishing, just as it did for thousands of years before. Everyone might own a snowmobile, but there are still dozens of dog teams staked out along the frozen coastline on the edge of the town. People wear modern high-tech winter coats, but seal skins are still stretched outside of homes, waiting to be turned into mukluks, the preferred winter boots of the Inuit. Surviving and existing on the land are still a very big part of their culture, so it's little wonder that the tenacity and ingenuity of the Inuit are shaped by the arctic landscape. That may sound like a cliché, but there is nothing cliché about it to those who call this place home. Barren, cold, and isolated, Pond Inlet plunges into near total darkness for months each year, before slowly emerging into the blinding light of early spring.

All my time was to be spent out on the land hunting with my Inuit guides. I knew there was nothing about this trip that I wasn't going to enjoy. One look at the breathtaking beauty of this landscape and I was glad I was here, no matter the purpose. So I was quite happy to hop on a snowmobile and head out for a long journey on the land. We loaded up komatiks (toboggans) full of supplies and gas, bundled up our bodies, and took to the trail, which was mostly out on the vast arctic sea ice with nothing more than the odd iceberg to break the wind.

To the Inuit, the land itself is their supermarket; that's where they prefer to go for sustenance. It's just a really big grocery store with a long way between aisles. Whatever modern tools they have are always put to use in getting out on the land. Our trip to the "grocery store" meant 24 hours of solid, full-speed snowmobile riding to hunt caribou and seal and to net for char. Along the way I discovered that even my guide, who had been hunting for years and looked to be in his late 50s or early 60s, had never tried eating the caribou fly larvae, written in the history books to be a traditional food source for the Inuit. After we had spent a couple of days successfully hunting three caribou, I made sure we tried it for the first time together. I laughed as my companions' grimaced faces twisted over the sour, rotten milk-like taste of the fly larvae. Even for me, it was kind of gross.

When we stopped many miles up a nameless river to fish through the ice with a net, we used a contraption that pushed the net a hundred feet under the ice to the hole at the other end. The device is of the same design that has existed for a thousand years, though now it's made out of wood instead of whalebone. We found the first of the two ice-fishing holes thanks to a pole that was sticking out of it, but my guide had a hard time finding the second one. It had been cut into the ice earlier in the season and maintained by passing fishermen, and he needed to find it since starting a new hole in the eight-foot-thick ice would be impossible. So Shiati simply pulled out his satellite phone and called his partner to find out the direction of the second hole. If he stretched the net out in that direction, it should land right on the spot. Modern technology saved the day of traditional net fishing.

As we traveled the land, I looked forward to bettering my igloo-building techniques with instruction from my guide, but was disappointed to learn that it was becoming a lost skill. Shiati taught me well anyway, and we constructed a pretty strong little igloo. Yet when pressed, he admitted that he hasn't stayed in one in at least 20 years. He says the skill is not really needed anymore because they always travel with heated tents. Igloo construction has been relegated to quaint speed-building contests at winter fairs. As I prepared to spend some time in our igloo, my guide headed back to his heated tent with its cot and cozy sleeping bag. The rest of the week, which was spent moving from one hunt to the next, culminated in my successful hunt of a seal (thanks to a high-powered and scoped-in rifle).

I have tasted seal eye before, and I just can't get anyone from the outside to believe me when I say it tastes good. This time, however, I once again had a captive audience, courtesy of my camera operator, Johnny. He bravely gave the eyeball a try—then quickly turned to puke. I'm not sure if it was the consistency or just the thought that got him, but I know that Laura, who was taking photographs, was holding back her own stomach at the thought alone. Or maybe it was the blood trickling down my hands as I squirted the gelatin from the inside of the eyeball into my mouth. I'm not sure what exactly got to her.

I don't think the Inuit look at the land as harsh and barren. They are a people rich in culture, a land-based culture. The Inuit show that it is not too late to reclaim their own culture and live by it, even after the loss of a spiritual belief system intrinsically tied to the earth. I envied their understanding of the land. I envied their simple lifestyle based on the movement of animals and fish. They were without ceremony, and yet they themselves seem to be the perfect example of a living bridge between the old ways and the new.

I am asked constantly what the grossest thing I ever had to eat while surviving was, yet rarely am I asked what my favorite survival food experience was! It's sun-dried arctic char. Having spent years eating everything from leeches and ants to snakes and turtles, I will never forget the elation I felt when I hauled in four large arctic char while surviving on the coast of Baffin Island. The technique for preparing the meat is so simple, yet it produces the most amazing sushi possible.

Intact at the tail but with the meat and skin separated from the rest of the body, the char is left hanging in the wind, sun, and sometimes smoke to dry slightly. The chunks of pink flesh are scored into squares that separate when the fish is hung so that they can properly dry on three sides. The result is the most delicious meal—I can only describe it as melt-in-your-mouth salmon cream cheese. Ironically, during that particular survival ordeal in the High Arctic, my *Survivorman* crew, a number of miles away, were not looked after well. They stayed in a tent heated by a smelly propane stove and ate horrible packaged soup while I kept a wood fire going all day and night and dined on fresh arctic sushi!

AYAHUASCA
The Huachipaeri

Being out on the land with the Inuit was enriching for me emotionally, physically, and spiritually, as time out on the land always is. Yet I still hadn't found what I was looking for. I had been given protection and preparation through the scarification ceremony and trance dancing in Africa. I experienced personal progress through my time with the Inuit and the seed ceremony in Madagascar. I struggled with the process in those ceremonies, not feeling; then feeling a little; then not feeling again. There was beauty and gentleness with the Sangoma in South Africa. There was intensity and belief instilled within me when the San performed their trance dance in the Kalahari Desert. With the Sea Gypsies I felt a connection to the land and water. I found darkness bordering on voodoo in the seed ceremony of the Antanosy in Madagascar. And there was simple adoration of the land and the animals with the Inuit in the High Arctic. But now I was heading to Peru, where the intensity of the ceremonies and potential for greater understanding, perhaps even enlightenment, could reach new heights. At least this is what I was hoping as I set out to work with shamans and take part in a variety of ceremonies meant to bring me into harmony with the earth and align my spirit to the natural world.

For the making of *Beyond Survival*, we circled the globe eight times in eight months. Traveling like that makes for a lot of great memories in the backseat of a Land Rover while driving on remote jungle and mountain roads. For this leg of the trip, we were on the mountain roads of the high Andes that you find once you leave the cultural beauty of Cusco, Peru, to travel downward into the Amazon jungle. Susceptible to constant mudslides, these are some of the most treacherous "drivable" roads on the planet. There were times we boogied along the twisting dirt paths that I could look out my window and down into a green abyss a few thousand feet deep. The edge of the road was a mere 12 inches from our tires. If someone ever went off the side, and it has happened, there would be no chance of finding them again. And there would be little chance of their survival.

As we left the cool, fresh air of elevations high enough to produce altitude sickness, the deep, dark dampness of the jungle became more apparent at each pit stop along our route. There were times we stopped to pee, times to check on the rest of the convoy, times to do some filming. But mostly there were times to stop because, on this ridiculously dangerous road with no room to pass, we often met trucks and cars traveling in the other direction. Inevitably, either they or we would have to slowly back up until there was a little spit of road one could pull into to offer a hair of room to pass. On the odd occasion, arguments broke out over who should do the backing up. The mudslides were usually not impassable, but there were plenty of times when we had to get a good run at it. A few of us were ready to jump out and help push the vehicle through, all the while looking over our shoulders at the deadly drop only feet away.

Finally we reached lower elevations, and the road started to flatten out when we arrived in a little town. We were not the first outsiders to drive through, but we were a spectacle. People watched us carefully from their doorways as slowly we drove through the center of town on the way to our little hotel. It was a dark feeling. Something went on here—something dark and sinister. We could just feel it.

I'm used to being stared at by remote peoples, but those are the looks of curiosity. Here we felt the stares of caution and self-guarding. It was a weird feeling. Then we saw something out in front of the dingy little buildings. A bunch of big tarps was laid out, each one covered with green coca leaves drying in the sun. These were the same leaves I had been chewing to help relieve altitude sickness since I landed in Cusco; the same leaves I had been drinking as tea, hoping for the same result. And, yes, the same leaves that are turned into cocaine. But these towns export them as "tea leaves," a legitimate and legal business that keeps everyone going economically. Every corner we rounded revealed another set of tarps on the ground with leaves drying.

There was a small airport on the edge of town, where mostly helicopters land. Our preproduction research had not turned up this airport ahead of time, which is too bad because it would have saved us the long drive down from Cusco. For some reason that I couldn't uncover, we were not allowed to fly into this airport. I wasn't even aware that it existed. Then I found out: it doesn't (nudge, nudge; wink, wink).

The cloak-and-dagger atmosphere continued to hang over the town, and later that night, as we sat around the dinner table of the only hotel around, the power went out. Apparently it goes out every night at the same time, 9 p.m. How amazing is that . . . a predictable power outage! And it always comes back on at 11 p.m. As it turns out, within that two-hour stretch the cocaine dealers make their move under the cover of darkness, transporting coca leaves en masse. This was a cocaine town, and my small crew and I were passing through to innocently make a documentary film. We kept to ourselves and stayed inside our little hotel compound. The next morning I walked over to the grouping of shops selling food, T-shirts, belts, and hats, where I bought a T-shirt sporting a picture of Peter Chris, the drummer from KISS. For me, the surreal experience of buying a shirt with a rock 'n' roll god on it, in the middle of the Amazon jungle where they exported leaves soon to be turned into cocaine, was too messed up to miss.

We got stuck in the mud more than a dozen times as we made our way up and down and across little streams on an extremely rough road on the way to the small jungle village where we would meet the Huachipaeri tribe. Every time the trucks got stuck and we had to get out to push, I'd run out into the jungle to drop my pants since I was suffering yet again from jungle food and traveler's belly. The village is in a small grass clearing about the size of a soccer field, where a half-dozen wooden houses and buildings all face toward the middle. In fact, before our time was over here, we would enjoy a big game of soccer against the Huachipaeri kids and men.

But for now the first order of the day was to accept a meal as guests. My crew and I gathered in the small wooden building that normally served as the school. Tables were set out so that we could meet and discuss what we would be doing for the coming week. To my delight they served yucca drink, which is prepared by old ladies who chew the yucca leaves and spit the mush back into a bowl to ferment. I always make sure my crew members are served up a bowl of the "old lady spit drink," whenever we come across it. Laura weaseled out. Having previously escorted me to the Amazon, she knew what it was. But Johnny, Andrew, and Peter were all fair game. The meat dish was alligator. For years my crew has joked about the disgusting things I have had to eat, so it was sweet revenge when I got the chance to see them, out of respect for the people we were visiting, have to swallow some pretty disagreeable fare.

Once again, the hunting and fishing techniques involved gathering an array of plant parts to make a poison. Before heading out, as an act of respect for the jungle, most of us were painted up with face markings for protection. Only my intrepid and agreeable cameraman Peter Esteves missed out on the paint, to his own folly. While out digging through the jungle floor for grubs and roots we had to be constantly on the alert for numerous species of ants with an extremely painful bite. Then, as we stood about getting some filming done, Peter began jumping around. He was being stung by wasps from the nest he had hit with his leg while he filmed. It was a curious-looking nest—the wasps themselves formed a ball the size of a melon by clinging to each other. So it looked like a black-moving ball hanging from a branch. What was interesting is that we were all standing there, and we had all moved that branch around—but none of us was stung. Immediately afterward, the women who had been leading me on this trek painted Peter up. It was too late, however, to protect his bruised ego.

This time, the stream where we were to place the poison was fairly fast-moving and shallow. I truly wondered how we were going to pull off this job. Wasn't the poison just going to wash away? Then it started. The entire village, it seemed, joined in to begin to block the flow of the river with hundreds of rocks. Once they had formed a rock "dam" across the 20-foot breadth of the river, they began to fill it in with branches and grass. I saw that they had blue plastic tarps with them but weren't using them. I asked them why, and they said they didn't want to show how they really did it for my cameras. I told them I was there only to get the truth and that I respected that they incorporated modern material into their land-based survival skills. They were happy with this explanation and we all pitched in to cover the rocks with the ugly blue tarp, which helped to dam up the river significantly. I am sure most film crews would not let them use the modern plastic, opting for the traditional-looking grass. But I always demanded authenticity in my film making for this series. After the poison was swished around in the calm pool of water created by the river damming, the fish began to rise up to the surface just as they did for the poison fishing in Sri Lanka. To this day, this particular land-based survival skill never ceases to amaze me in its effectiveness. And it feels far more in harmony with the earth than does using dynamite to kill fish as is done in the "civilized" world.

The lives of the Huachipaeri revolve around ceremonies. Those I met did nothing without first performing a ceremony, usually asking for a good hunt, blessings, or permission from Pacha Mama (Mother Earth). Each ceremony uses plant items, feathers, rocks, or plant medicines. Arrows are rubbed with powerful plants to ensure better aim. The skin is colored for protection while in the jungle.

The jungle is a very dangerous place in many ways. There are more poisonous critters and plants than you can count, so no matter how experienced the Huachipaeri may be, they always enter with trepidation. And without the ceremonies, it would be as if they were daring the spirits of the jungle to take them on. For the Huachipaeri, that would be too risky.

I always honor my role in such ceremonies by being "present" and fully taking part. If I don't, then I have no right to be there. As it turns out, these jungle inhabitants didn't even want me to attempt survival out in the jungle without properly preparing through ceremony. They believe that working with the spirits of the land keeps things in balance and harmonious. They needed to align my spirit with the spirits of rock, wind, water, fire, and the jungle and earth itself. Without these ceremonies, people are not living their lives in harmony with nature. And living in harmony with nature is what will help the human species survive throughout the coming century.

The last of the many ceremonies was the sacred tobacco ceremony. But before we could take part in it, we first had to light a sacred fire. The tricky part is that it had to be started by hand drill—no easy feat in a dry desert, let alone a damp jungle. But since the fire was sacred, we couldn't use any old matches.

In some ways, I think this fire-starting, which took hours and hours of everyone working together, was another example of my inner struggle to part the veil that separated me from clearer insight. The jungle is damp, and hand drills are a tough way to get a fire going. Four of us labored over the spinning of the skinny spindle to try to create enough friction for fire. If we couldn't do it, it would be a bad omen and my companions might have felt they didn't want to continue on working with me. For my part it seemed another example of how spiritual breakthroughs don't come easily for me.

In fact, maybe nothing in life comes easily for me. I seem always to search out the hardest way to do just about anything, and fire-starting in the middle of the jungle served as a metaphor for what I was experiencing—emotionally, spiritually, and psychologically—throughout my journey. I was becoming worried when finally, well into the darkness of night, we got our fire. I had been skeptical when we started to spin the wood. I was skeptical as we worked over it, just as much of my mind remains skeptical about matters of the spirit. But finally we got the fire going, with a bit of help from the other two men. Perhaps this perseverance and the combining of human energies was an indication of a breakthrough yet to come.

The tobacco ceremony, which was meant to honor the spirits of the forest plants, was also meant to clear and cleanse. And that it did. Some would describe the feeling as a spike being hammered up your nose. The shaman, Alberto, used a double-ended pipe. A tobacco and ground bark mixture was placed in the pipe but not lit. It was a kind of snuff. The shaman gently blew in one end, with my nose above the other end of the pipe. As gently as he blew, it still hit me hard. The shamans are so used to it they use a curved pipe to blow into their own noses.

You don't get stoned or feel anything like that, but you achieve an incredible sense of clarity. Then the nausea of the tobacco kicks in, and it becomes pretty difficult not to throw up. One of my interpreters puked. Even my camera crew got involved. The smokers didn't get the nausea, but the rest of us did. Clarity of vision and clarity of the mind don't always come without some kind of pain. We may have appeared like a small group of people sitting around sniffing snuff from a pipe, but the appearance is where any similarity ended.

I had greatly looked forward to taking the "plant medicine" in my next ceremony thanks to all I had learned about it through my research. It took my shaman a few days just to gather all the medicinal plants that make up the special drink mixture known as ayahuasca. And it was imperative that I do the gathering with him. This was a powerful cleansing ritual that was not to be taken lightly. Nothing about taking this medicine said "catch a buzz." The whole point of the medicine and the ceremony was to align my spirit with the earth. There were plants to align my spirit to other plants; plants to purge me of ailments and disease, congestion, and even evil. The plants were meant to bring me into harmony with the earth energy and the spirits of the natural world. So the energy of "me," the plants, and the earth all had to align, which is why it was important that I did the picking.

In all, the collection of plants for the drink included more than 14 different species. That's 14 different plant spirits joining together to create a powerful experience. Combined wrongly and the drink could

be poisonous. If the plants were gathered or prepared incorrectly, or if even my intentions were wrong, then physical, psychological, or spiritual harm could come to me. The whole process was in no way just about the medicine. The ceremony was everything. It was all about personal intention. This drink was meant to show me a path to greater understanding.

In the dark of the hut that evening, we spent at least an hour relaxing and eating coca leaves. It was a dome-shaped, thatched-roof hut that was crawling with cockroaches. The floor was dirt, and light came from only a couple candles. The shaman smoked rolled cigarettes, lending the atmosphere a hazy look. This was a healing ritual called *la purga*, in which I was to physically purge all my demons and everything that I didn't need in my life. This ceremony, depending on the strength of the medicine and the intentions of the participant, is for purging all aspects of what it means to be human—physically, emotionally, mentally, and spiritually.

At first, the medicine caused me to throw up and purge jungle parasites. My vision went into a white light. Then I drank some more and tried to focus my intentions. I threw up again. But nothing hugely profound happened, at least as far as I could tell. My skeptical side began to emerge again, and in my mind I debated what I was feeling. I felt myself actually *trying* hard to feel *something*. Then my inner voice asked, "Why should I be trying at all? Why isn't it just happening?" I had heard so much about ayahuasca and its ability to help you see into yourself. Yet I still wasn't feeling much of anything other than nausea. What was happening subconsciously, I didn't know. It is taught that the spirit of ayahuasca is the spirit of a grandmother. Perhaps she just wasn't ready for me to meet her yet.

Hours later, the ayahuasca ceremony was complete and we left the hut to sleep. Once again, I was feeling let down. At this point, my crew expected so much that I didn't have the heart to tell them that I felt so little. I was told that the medicine of the shaman, Alberto, wasn't a "strong" medicine; that it was meant to be weaker to encourage purging. I think the medicine itself decided that I wasn't ready for a strong kick in the ass. Perhaps I needed more work. In hindsight, this medicine ceremony was one more piece of my personal puzzle over who I was and what my purpose in life is. It was going to take something else—more processing—to get me to break past my own skepticism.

PACHA MAMA
The Incans

I walked into the hotel in Cusco and made my way over to the ever-available coca tea. They tell you to drink it constantly or chew the leaves to relieve altitude sickness, though the chewing can make you feel nauseous. Too often travelers turn their noses up at local customs, figuring they know better or they have Western pills that will win the day. I'll stick to trusting the locals.

Cusco is one of the nicest cities I have ever visited. The ancient Incan stonework still lines some of the streets, and by just touching the stones you can feel the past. It is an architecturally beautiful place with friendly people and a deep, rich history. If you ever want to visit a place where the food in every restaurant is outstanding, then Cusco is the place to go. The central square, a tradition of city planning that North American urban designers unfortunately overlook, is a wonderful place full of people, musicians, shops, restaurants, and more. Indeed, on this evening two dogs were mating in the middle of the square, fully locked. I had to explain it to a woman passing by who thought something was wrong with them. The dogs didn't seem to mind.

The musicianship in the local bands was outstanding. Six or more musicians would cram onto a tiny stage in a local eatery and play a variety of instruments like their lives depended on it. From the first to the last beat of any given song, the members were focused, playing their instruments with feverish intensity. They whooped and hollered and harmonized their way through piece after piece. They sang songs praising Pacha Mama and would have made proud fans of rock bands like Phish or Widespread Panic.

Cusco has its dark side, too. Everywhere you turn there are the leftover signs of the oppressive Spanish occupation. Even the inquisition rooms are still intact in the basements of some churches. Life-sized statues of Jesus nailed to the cross—replete with blood dripping out of his wounds—are everywhere. All of it is over-the-top gothic Catholicism that left a dark feeling in the pit of my stomach. I had lyrics from a Neil Young song called "Cortez the Killer" (though another Spaniard conquered the Incas) playing in my head as I strolled the streets. In one spot, the foundation the Incan people built so long ago remains intact, while the churches built on top of it were destroyed by earthquakes three separate times.

Every location I go to film usually requires someone familiar with the local customs and laws, someone who has deep contacts within the region. Jahkey and Delia were my tag team duo for this trip to Peru. Jahkey is an incredibly personable man, slight in stature but big in heart, the kind of guy who makes you feel warm when he smiles at you or hugs you. He lives in New York but was here to help and work with Delia, the woman who arranged for my journeys with the Huachipaeri Tribe and the ayahuasca ceremony.

Both Delia and Jahkey were wonderfully upbeat and two of the nicest local fixers (people who make all the local arrangements for film crews) I had worked with. Delia and I hit it off because of her filmmaking background and desire to share the beauty of the South American culture with the world through film. Jahkey and I connected over music. I have been building a major concert tour involving world music; he, too, has been working with indigenous musicians to capture as many of them in recordings as possible. But then why shouldn't these two be nice people? They spend their lives learning from earth masters like the Inca and taking part in ceremonies meant to align their very souls with the energy of the earth and the spirit of all things.

Jahkey motioned over to a man sitting on the hotel couch in full Incan regalia. This man was Kucho, the Inca high priest who was to take me on the journey that would change my life forever. Like Incan people generally, Kucho is short and dark. I had never met him before, but he walked over and gave me a warm hug. Sure, it must be a tradition, and perhaps I'm just being idealistic. But there seemed to be something more in his hugs. I get great hugs from North Americans, too. But Kucho almost communicated something to me with his physical act of hugging. He held on longer than most people would.

Before I could continue on my journey of personal and spiritual discovery in the high Andes Mountains, I needed to confirm my permission from Mother Earth. And although I was there to film *Beyond Survival*, I felt different. There was nothing about my intentions that said "TV show" or "tourist endeavor." I approached every action and every ceremony with respect and honesty. I made a conscious effort to become a bridge between the world of filmmaking and my own personal spiritual enlightenment. But it was not an easy balance to strike. I was feeling ready to experience, to feel, to understand more than I ever had. But my stubborn and skeptical personality needed a catalyst. I needed something to part the veil of understanding, to wash away all the intangible heady musings, and to link the two worlds of spiritual and pragmatic intentions. I needed medicine from the earth to open the door of my mind and heart while ego and reason took a backseat.

We hopped in the van and headed out to the Peruvian countryside, a place equally rich in culture and history. Here the hillsides are dotted with sacred Incan sites with romantic names like the Temple of the Snake. Here hilltops and mountaintops are aligned in geometric patterns that ancient wisdom takes into account for ceremonies. And here, among all the sacred sites and "power stones," people go about their simple daily lives.

Yet for all this power, we weren't going to Machu Picchu. It's not that Machu Picchu isn't a special place. For regardless of the tourists, it is a place of high energy and was built for reasons only the ancient Incas knew. It still seems to emanate powerful energy. If you are open to it, you may even be able to feel its power in your soul.

We were heading to a place where the tourists don't go, a small hillside dotted with Incan ceremonial sites. On the hill is a cave where I would experience a ceremony that represented my leaving of the womb of Pacha Mama and moving into a new beginning. Here also was a small waterfall for cleansing and offerings. The Temple of the Moon was here, too. These temples and stones were smoothed over by thousands of caring Incan hands that worked them into shapes and steps over many years.

First we performed a short ceremony of permission at the water. We then continued up the mountain to a flat area at the top, where I saw a conspicuous flat boulder just big enough to lie on. With Kucho was his small daughter, who looked to be about 6 or 7 years old. She would perform the ceremony with her father, the master. I don't know if it was tradition or if she was in training, but her involvement lent a beautiful lightness of being to the process. I was, for only a second, taken aback when Kucho instructed her to hold my hand as we walked up the grassy hillside. Her warm little fingers tucked in mine and made me lonely for my own daughter back at home. I wondered if it was his attempt to calm me and make me relax. If it was, it worked.

Various ceremonial accoutrements were set out on a woven mat. A *despacho*—a thank you to Pacha Mama and request of permission to the spirits of the earth and Pacha Mama herself—was performed. A ceremony like this always requires a *despacho* out of respect. It was not new or uncomfortable to me. I never felt awkward because, in a sense, I've been performing permission requests my whole life. Even when simply surviving in the bush, I silently asked permission of the trees or spoke my gratitude to them when I needed to cut them down to make a shelter. I never questioned my desire to do so. It just always seems that thanking the forest, the trees, the rocks, the animals, and the water is the right thing to do, especially if I'm about to take their life energy and use it for myself. The Incan people simply turned their gratitude to the greater spirit of Mother Earth.

HOURS OF CEREMONIES had already taken place over the past three-quarters of a year, and there would be more. So many of the ceremonies I film never make it on to the TV series, since the networks want to showcase land skills and survival stuff. It's disappointing for me, because I feel the magic ingredient of what I do in the wilderness is missing. I want my viewers to understand the secret behind my success: respect and love for the land, and gratitude to the spirits that allow me to survive at all.

After the *despacho* was performed it was time for a ceremony known as Huachuma, so Kucho handed me a small shot of a green liquid known as San Pedro. I had no idea how it was processed, only that it's from a cactus of that name. Since Kucho is an Incan high priest, he has special permission from the Peruvian government to gather San Pedro from the side of the Machu Picchu Mountain. I was told that although a large glass of this medicine is often given when the drink comes from other sources, I would need only a small shot. This was powerful stuff, so just a little would be enough.

Kucho continued to chant and sing over me while his daughter continuously fanned a feather over my head and body. An hour went by and he asked me how I felt. I felt nothing really. Kucho decided to administer another small glass of the San Pedro. I lay back on the flat rock while the chanting and singing continued. Since he was to accompany me on my journey, Kucho also had drunk two small shots of San Pedro.

At one point an eagle flew above us. It circled overhead, but not directly; it seemed to be unwilling to circle over my entire body. The eagle made its circular passes in the sky just above the top of my head—nearly touching it. Kucho watched and said the eagle represented understanding. He said the spirit world was trying to reach me, but it was clear that I held on to a stubborn skepticism. In other words, I was a tough nut to crack. For Kucho, this insight was drawn from the observation that the eagle wouldn't circle over my full body. Not yet, anyway.

Then it began.

As the camera crew slowly and respectfully scuttled about trying to get a different angle of me on the rock, I began to hear a voice whispering my name. The camera team's activities became fuzzier and more distant. I paid no attention to the crew, something that was out of character for me. But, as in the seed ceremony in Madagascar, I didn't care; the voice beckoned. First it was very distant, but slowly coming toward me—as when someone speaks to you when you are sleeping. The sounds become part of your dream, but then you wake up and the voice is entirely physical. Then it was with me, hovering right beside me and speaking directly in my ear. It was a woman's voice—soft and clear, firm and comforting.

I have never hidden the fact that I had a misspent youth in the suburbs of Toronto, drinking beer and taking drugs. If I am a role model as I am sometimes considered by groups such as the Boy Scouts, it is precisely because I pulled myself out of all that waste and made a life for myself. So with that in mind, I can say that I know what it's like to be high. I know the hallucinogenic effects of wild mushrooms and the like. But this was clearly not that sensation. This effect was audible and about to become a clear, vivid, and tangible conversation. It was not out loud for the others to hear, but it may as well have been, as far as how I heard it. The whole point of this medicine was to open up a conversation with Pacha Mama. Some cultures use vision quests and dreams prompted by abstention from food and water for days on end. Some use meditation and concentration and prayer. Some use plant medicine. I have been too stubborn to master meditation, and I have yet to properly experience a dream vision quest. So here I was, the participant in a plant medicine ceremony meant to reintroduce me to the powerful energy of the earth we call Mother Nature. Mother Earth. Pacha Mama. I say "reintroduce" because, as we spoke, I realized that I had been having a conversation with her all my life. I had always felt her speak to me, but until that day I had never been able to hear her with such certainty and clarity.

The conversation went something like this:

"Les, you have known me always. When you used to lie on rocks and fall asleep beside the rivers, you were laying your head on my skin. When you used to kiss the rock before getting up and continuing on your journey, you were kissing me. I know how deeply you loved me, and you showed it. But you have needed to be away. And I am so glad you have found me again. I will always be here for you. I have never left, but you have returned to me and now we shall never be apart."

So I questioned her. Even now my skeptical side was strong. First I issued a challenge. "How do I know this is real, and I'm not just high?" I asked.

"Try and move your legs," she said. I tried and could not. Now she had my attention.

Then she said, "Okay, now try and move them." And I could.

So she said, "Do you need more proof?"

Then I began to ask her questions. I asked, "But in knowing you . . . what does this do to my understanding of the greater consciousness, of God, of Jesus, of all the spiritual masters and teachings?"

She replied, "Ah yes. Jesus knows me too."

I asked her more questions and gave her more challenges. I needed to be sure this wasn't just some different kind of high. And every answer she gave me seemed so perfect. I had no urge to say, "Yeah, but!"—which would be my normal way.

I don't know how long I lay there and conversed with her. It felt like hours. It felt like seconds. Time stood still for me. And this connection, this warmth, this understanding permeated my very being. When others speak of similar experiences, they often say they can't describe what they saw or heard. But I could. It was as clear as day.

Then I began to ask her my purpose. Why was I here? What was the point? What was *my* point?

That's when she confirmed everything that had been coming at me for years. That's when she told me something that encapsulated my very being, what my life's efforts had been about.

"You are a bridge," she said

Until this point, from nobody—not an elder, not a shaman, and not in a dream—had I heard the word that would ring so clearly to me, the title that made such perfect sense. I had often wondered why I was making these films, why I had become Survivorman, why I was in this position of influence and understanding. I was no one special. But these experiences keep coming my way; this life keeps getting bigger and bigger.

And then she said it again: "Les, you are a bridge. You exist perfectly between the two worlds, the two questions, the two forms of consciousness. Stop fighting it; embrace it. It is what you are about. It is who you are. I am in pain. I am hurting and I need help. You can speak my cry for help to the world." I was emotional to the point of tears. I was overwhelmed, though in a good way. It was a warm sensation, nothing that scared me.

As the effects of the San Pedro began to mellow, she did not leave. And that connection was not severed and did not fade. And to this day it hasn't diminished. The medicine was supposed to open a conversation with Pacha Mama. Well, it did that. It was never said that it would stop after the medicine had passed through my physical system. That's what happens when you're high. Eventually it all stops and you come "down." But since I had not been "high," there was no place to come down from. I simply had a conversation.

It was about parting the veil. It was about connecting beyond this physical realm, like the San and the Antanosy do with trancing. What North American aboriginals are able to do with vision quests and the monks are able to do with meditation, the Inca do with plant medicine. And knowing my personality, it was the right place for me to be. It was the method that fit the person rather than the person trying to fit the method, for there is not only one way to journey the soul and go beyond this physical existence. The wand must choose the wizard as it were. As there are many different types of personalities, there are different types of communicating in a metaphysical sense. And this communication taught me and put a name to what I was. Or at least to what I could perhaps be: a bridge.

APUS MOUNTAIN SPIRITS

Incan High Priest

If taking part in the Huachuma ceremony parted a veil that once hid understanding and clarity from me, then the next journey was to be a test of my newfound enlightenment. With the scarification, trance dancing, devil dancing, and Cumoutin ceremonies, I was witnessing and taking part in activities never before seen by outsiders, let alone filmed and photographed. Now I was about to take a trek never before experienced by an outsider. I would become an Ukuku, something no white outsider had ever been allowed to be.

The Ukukus are the Peruvian warrior guardians of Mother Earth. They are part of the Q'uero heritage, the Q'ueros themselves being direct descendants of the Incas. Once a year, more than a hundred thousand people climb to the valley of Sinakara in the Peruvian Andes to take part in the Q'ollorit'i festival, which has so many twists and turns that it's hard to put your finger on what it celebrates. By my estimation, the Q'ollorit'i festival offers a chance to bring all your dreams to Lord of Q'ollorit'i, the spirit of the mountain. It also encourages the young Q'uero men to prove themselves worthy of protecting Mother Earth and to fulfill the sacred responsibilities of the Ukuku warrior. Lastly, it provides an opportunity to view the "rock of Jesus," where it is believed Christ left his image.

Elizabeth Jenkins is a remarkable individual. American born, her experience with the Incan people is unsurpassed. Though she is primarily an author, she now lives in Hawaii growing macadamia nuts and providing cultural exchanges for young Q'uero children. She has written many books on Incan prophecies and has taken too many metaphysical journeys to count. Clearly, I respect her tremendously, so when she agreed to help me enter the world of the Ukukus—the world of the Incan high priests and Lord of Q'ollorit'i high atop the Andes Mountains—I was ecstatic.

The structure of my journey seemed simple enough. Walk 100 miles *uphill* through the high Andes on a trek with a man named Don Humberto, who comes from a long line of Incan high priests. The Andes is the longest and one of the highest mountain ranges in the world, so even our lowest altitude would be about 12,000 feet, though we would climb to 17,000 feet during the trek. The potential for altitude sickness is high, and our oxygen-starved lungs served as a constant reminder. Like I said: simple!

The purpose of the trek through the mountain passes would be to cleanse and prepare me to join the Ukukus at the festival and then to become one of them. Don Humberto was to perform many sacred *despachos* and ceremonies along the way to place power into me and prepare me for the final destination. There he would pass me to the Ukukus, who had made their own trek up the other side of the mountain.

Once I joined the Ukukus (I'd be wearing an Ukuku costume made of alpaca fur, complete with a woolen mask to hide my identity), we would climb up to the sacred glacier to receive the blessings of Lord of Q'ollorit'i. Somewhere along the way we would have to engage in bullwhip battles meant to test our strength and keep us warm on the cold glacial ice. We would then descend the glacier and return to the masses below.

But before any of this could begin, Elizabeth said I must go through some important ceremonies right here in the Cusco area. Imagine my smile when we stopped the van at the very same sacred Incan rock site that I had just been to for the Huachuma ceremony the week before. Clearly the Incan people highly respected this place as one of great power and significance. This time, however, our destination was the small stone temples I had walked past last week.

As always, we were to start with a *despacho* to ask for permission and blessings from Mother Earth. Before that happened, though, Don Humberto gave me a small woven square of material inside which I was to keep my personal pieces of power. This was not about souvenirs and keepsakes; Don Humberto wanted to transfer earth energy and power into my *despacho* collection. In fact, the entire crew was asked to take part in the ceremony and given similar *despacho* pouches.

Elizabeth made it clear that, for the ceremony to be a success, our personal intentions had to be pure and based on a foundation of love and acceptance. If they weren't—and especially if they were malevolent in any way—we wouldn't be permitted to continue. I cast an eye to Andrew, who is skeptical at the best of times but is respectful enough to go through the motions to honor the situation. Some of my other camera operators are often profoundly moved and brought to tears during these ceremonies.

A ceremony was to take place in a long and narrow cave. I entered it and, as instructed, curled up high and tight into the back corner. The idea was that I was to mentally pass through time in my mind: back through my years; back through my childhood; back into the womb until I was standing in front of my father and mother as they first met. I was supposed to relive how I felt about everything in life along each step of the psychological journey. Any hurt and pain must be forgiven and released, joys relived and released until I was back to being just a soul, a new being. Then—and only then—was I to exit the cave, which represented the womb of Mother Earth. She would be my new mother; my life was to begin again.

Half sitting, half lying down, and curled up in a ball against the farthest corner of the smooth rock walls, I focused diligently and tried to forget about time (and the half-dozen people waiting outside with video cameras). Once again I gave all the respect and honoring I could. I wasn't broken down with any kind of emotional release, as you might expect. I wasn't moved to tears. And, yet, there was a little of what I call a "letting go," some kind of release. I was even able to run my camera and record my internal reactions to it all, so I could act as a link between the two worlds of spiritual enlightenment and practical filmmaking.

When I finally emerged from the cave, we carried on and closed off the day without fanfare; this was a personal and internal journey. Interestingly, though, I felt more attached in understanding to Don Humberto than to my friends and crew. Sure, I was aware of our professional filmmaking duties, but I wanted to connect spiritually and continue working on that area of my personal life. Part of me simply wished the cameras were not here. As it is so often the case in my life, I was concentrating on film-making when I would have been better served to live the experience alone.

With the *despachos*, the various cleansing ceremonies, and the rebirthing complete, Don Humberto was now ready to take me on the traditional journey through the mountains. Before this journey began, Elizabeth confided in me that Don Humberto would have pulled the plug if he thought my intentions were not honorable. Without knowing it, I was being judged and tested, watched and considered. Not in a harsh or negative way; Don Humberto simply knew that the path I was about to take was an impor-tant one. It was much deeper than I could know.

Like all the teachers, shamans, and high priests I had encountered before him, Don Humberto said, "You are on a great journey. One that is important to the world. You will have great influence." He put his hand on my shoulder and peered deep into my eyes as he spoke. Like many others before him, Don Humberto knew nothing of my TV shows or who I was outside of his world.

We gathered at the end of a long drive near the beginning of a mountain pass. We were a large and cluttered group: three camera operators, Elizabeth and her friend and assistant Chrystalle, Fredy our Q'uero interpreter, and Don Humberto and his two associate high priests. Add all our camera and camp gear for traveling through the mountains, and it was clear why we needed 29 horses for the journey! Since the horses were so small, Andrew and I decided that we would walk the entire journey, using our horses as pack-horses only. At six-foot-four, Andrew could stand on the ground while sitting on the horse.

After a couple of days of mountain trekking, we were to make it to the village where Don Humberto was born and raised. Even today the village is shrouded in mystery; people in the lower elevations talk about it as a legend. It seems the Q'uero were able to survive there during the Spanish occupation because it was considered too high and remote for the invaders to bother with. So the Spanish never found the village, and its residents were left alone until an anthropologist discovered them in the 1950s. That's why the Incan traditions live on here. (It's often been debated if the people were found or if they chose to be found at that time.)

Along our route we were lucky to see small herds of government-protected vicuñas, an animal that resembles the alpaca but is smaller and with longer fur. One scarf knitted from their hair costs $800 on the North American market. So they are herded and kept alive to have their hair shorn. Shortly after spotting the vicuñas, we had a nasty situation when the pack of one of the horses slipped to its side and down to its belly. The animal immediately panicked and went running off into the hillside with important gear getting trampled under its hooves. On another occasion, Johnny's horse spooked, sending Johnny flying off its back. It's not a problem, as long as you don't mind that the grassland was studded with jagged rocks.

As we reached the height of the pass we still had a long journey to Don Humberto's village. The wet snow whipped in our faces while we looked down with every step for fear of twisting or breaking an ankle on the loose rocks. Don Humberto said the mountain spirits were testing us, making sure we were pushing through with the right intentions and wiping us clean of pretense and ego. It felt like a test.

The power in the mountains was palpable. But then there is always great power in mountains. You cannot help but be in awe of the energy of a mountain range. Elizabeth explained that each mountain has its own spirit, an Apu as she called it. These powerful spirits can decide at any minute to make your life a living hell. Therefore we needed to ask permission as we passed from mountain to mountain, Apus to Apus. The priests even played their flutes as they climbed. It was their way of constantly asking permission to be there and for safety in our travels.

This power is reciprocal, cycling from Pacha Mama and the Apus to the people, but also from the people back to Pacha Mama and the Apus. This reciprocity is what keeps the people alive in an otherwise harsh environment.

ALL TOO OFTEN when respect is not given and permission not requested, dark things happen to the offenders. People die inexplicably after desecrating sacred sites. There is a sacred rock site in Northern Ontario where pictographs (ancient Indian paintings) can be seen on a rock face above the waters of a remote lake. On one occasion, two drunken men went out of their way to disrespect the site by mocking it and trying to take a chunk of the painted rock as a souvenir. Within three weeks, both men died in separate incidents. Call it coincidence if you will, but stories like this one abound when it comes to sacred sites around the world. Conversely, good fortune falls on those who respect and honor the spirit world. The Inca people understand that this reciprocity is so vital that the survival of the earth also depends on it. The earth and the people need each other for survival. How profoundly true.

We finally reached Don Humberto's village—Qolpa Kucho—which is believed to be between six hundred and one thousand years old. It seemed dark and damp—just a tiny cluster of four or five stone structures housing a couple of families. They were alpaca herders.

Their lives revolved around the alpaca, which provides clothing and is a source of food. In a reciprocal arrangement that seems typical of these high Andean–dwelling people, the alpaca, too, rely on the safety of the village surroundings for nighttime protection from their natural predator, the pumas (mountain lion) that live in nearby hills. As the dark begins to settle on the village, all the alpacas instinctively know to come in from the surrounding hills to spend the night tucked in tightly against the stone houses. Were it not for the Incan people, the alpacas might have become extinct. Indeed, the Spanish actually tried to extirpate them to control the Incan people down in the valleys. They assumed that removing the alpaca would force the Andean people to become dependent and, eventually, slaves to the Spanish.

Elizabeth was a welcome visitor. She was known to these people because she had been traveling here for years to further her own connection to the Incan life. They were thrilled to see her again. In fact, she was actually going to be a godmother to a young couple who had waited five years for Elizabeth to return so that they could be married in her presence. This trip was to be the time. It was a double honor to be there with Don Humberto and to witness a traditional Incan wedding.

While the crew set up their tents, I was introduced to Rosa and her children. It seemed I would have the great honor of boarding inside their stone house. Rosa was pleasant and timid and said nothing, but she often smiled when she looked at me as she stirred something in a pot over the inside fire. I'm not sure about the Q'uero people's eyesight. Rosa's house was typically dark and smoky. It would have been terribly damp and musty, too, were it not for the small, constant fire.

Building fires isn't as easy as you'd think in a place like this, since there is no wood up here. As such, the Q'uero have to make the odd journey with packhorses four hours *down* to the tree line to gather firewood. It's amazing to me that, given the bounty in the Amazon jungle below, the Q'uero still choose to live way up here, on the top of a mountain in the mist and dull light, walking on ground that rarely if ever dries, sleeping, eating, and escaping the mountain weather in dark stone buildings. They likely know little of the outside world. Life for them is herding alpacas for subsistence.

The Q'uero may be remote but small influences creep in from time to time. Occasionally some of the men travel to a town in need of a shovel or other supplies. Or, although rare, a visitor like Elizabeth passes through and leaves some supplies or something for the children.

And so it was that I found a baby's doll with no arms or legs lying there in the mud. It was creepy in one sense, but fun in another. I took it to be my mascot and tied it to the back of my pack to journey with me across the mountain range. Today, it sits in my office in Canada—still kind of creepy, still kind of cute.

I pulled the heavy alpaca blanket over my head and fell asleep searching for air that wasn't filled with smoke and listening to the gentle scraping of Rosa's carved wooden spoon as she dragged it against a metal pot full of alpaca soup. She hovered close to the fire pit, which was built into the outside wall. With no chimney in the house, the air was thick; the smoke eventually made its way out of the thatched roof.

I took Rosa to be in her thirties. She never seemed to sleep. She just stirred the pot. I may have been the only white man she had ever seen, and definitely was the first white man to sleep in her house. We sensed an awkward feeling about my sleeping alone in the house, so after a time Laura joined me. She curled up beside me under the alpaca blanket, and together we searched for fresh air to breathe. Tomorrow was to be a very big day. Not only were we to travel into the hills to perform some important ceremonies, but the wedding was to take place that evening, too.

And an Incan wedding means an Incan wedding party.

For one of the ceremonies, we had only a short walk to another plateau. This ceremony was meant to bring me into harmony with the earth as well as enabling me to bring that harmony to others. I would be infused with power. When we got to the plateau, the first thing I noticed was a small, ice-cold mountain pond filled with meltwater from sacred glaciers.

At first the high priests needed time on their own to prepare with the spirits. As I joined them, I was instructed to strip down to my pants, with my boots off. This ceremony seemed to be one of cleansing and infusing with power. As if on cue, as I stood shirtless and wet, having just been doused with water by the priest, the weather became more intense. The wind and snow blew during what seemed to be a key point in the ceremony. Then, just as suddenly, the wind stopped and the sun shone down on me. Don Humberto and the other priests were watching the signs of nature closely to see if I was accepted or rejected. It certainly appeared to me as if these priests were invoking the energy of the wind, sun, snow, and rain, if not actually making commandments to them. Elizabeth explained that the true Incan priests, those who are so deeply in touch with Pacha Mama, have the ability to talk to the spirits of the wind and clouds. They can command the clouds to arrive or leave with nothing more than a wave of their hands.

Every step along the journey and every ceremony along the way represented another opportunity for the spirits to refuse me and for Don Humberto to turn me away. I wasn't sure what Don Humberto was leading me through with all these ceremonies, so I did what seemed natural: I acted on trust. As always, I approached each new experience with respect and honor. Otherwise, why bother being there at all?

After a wonderful wedding celebration that night on the misty mountain, we traveled to another glacial lake, which the locals believe to be filled with powerful feminine energy from the spirit Anusta. My task, at 6 o'clock in the high mountain morning, was to strip naked and immerse my body in the lake. This immersion would clean my entire store of energy and infuse me with power. No outsider has ever done this sacred ceremony (or any of the other ceremonies, for that matter). It was, apparently, all part of becoming an Ukuku warrior.

It did not come without risk. On occasion, some initiates have slipped into the cold water and been unable to pull themselves out, drowning in the process. As if he read my mind, Don Humberto looked at me moments before I began to disrobe. He said I was about to do a dangerous thing, and he did not want Anusta to consume me. So he told me not to jump in fully, but to slip in gently.

As he spoke, my fears immediately evaporated and I knew everything would be fine. Until that moment, I had a deep-seated fear of jumping in over my head in this pale, translucent green water at the foot of its glacier. I've done frigid water jumps before, but something was different here; I could feel it. Fully naked in the cold mountain mist, I gently stepped down onto some slippery rocks and immersed my body in the water. It was not a light-hearted experience like a polar bear swim on New Year's Day with a bunch of friends. It was reverent, but surprisingly painful. As a result of my years of dog-sledding and cold-weather survival, I suffer from Raynaud's phenomenon, a physiological reaction that causes the capillaries in my fingers and toes to close off in an attempt to save the rest of my body from hypothermia whenever I get cold. It's not generally a problem because I usually sort of shake the blood back into my extremities. But this time the pain was excruciating.

I looked down into the pale green water and could not see bottom, then realized why someone could quickly succumb to the cold and slip into oblivion in the deep waters. But I climbed out of the lake feeling cleansed and joined the high priests in the grass on the shore. I shook terribly as I put my clothes back on while they prayed and chanted and sung over me. My fingers and toes hurt so much that Don Humberto himself seemed to take pity on me as he bent down to tie my boots.

Now finished with the ceremony, we went back up the hill to our camp, where one of the other priests approached me. This was Francisco Apaza, a past president of the Qu'ero nation. He came in close and held me, all the while looking at me straight in the eyes and holding my gaze. He was neither somber nor celebratory, just dead serious. He said I needed to understand that whether I felt it or not, a great power had just been put into me and would not leave. It was more power than I could imagine. He said I should always remember that. What do you say to something like that? His words gave me confidence and helped me to internalize what had just happened.

The rest of the journey on the way to the Q'ollorit'i festival was a breathtaking trek through the mountain passes, one in which we were always asking permission and leaving offerings. Walking through the high Andes (Andrew and I had not given up on our deal to walk the entire journey) was worth a thousand photographs, every one of them postcard worthy. The view was magical in every sense. We traveled along narrow paths flattened against the sides of mountains, gazed down on mist-shrouded valleys, and gawked at sun-speckled hillsides. Dressed in ponchos and holding on to horse reins, we looked very much the part of an Incan mountain journey.

And then, finally, we were there. We pushed with our horses over a height of land and before us, in the valley far below, were more than a hundred thousand people on pilgrimage. Thousands of blue plastic tarps stretched out in every direction, a makeshift city surrounded by the distant echo of music and people. Don Humberto was sitting by himself a few hundred yards down on a rock, taking in the scene: the Q'ollorit'i festival.

12

Q'OLLORIT'I
The Ukukus

Having arrived at the Andean mountain festival known as the Q'ollorit'i, I had a moment to catch my breath at the peak of the mountain and ponder the view below. More than a hundred thousand people were down there, all of them bringing their dreams and desires to Lord of Q'ollorit'i, the lord of the mountain, to ask for them to be granted. They believe that if they honor the mountain spirit with prayers and supplications, Lord of Q'ollorit'i will make their dreams come true. Looming above them all were three different glaciers, each considered sacred by the Inca.

The festival is also known today as Qoyllur R'iti—Qoyllur means "star," and R'iti means "snow"—so people call it the Star Snow festival. It is a meaningful title because the festival also marks the return of the Pleiades constellation in the winter sky. The festival celebrates the rise of the Pleiades, which is related to crops and planting. It also takes place at the site of a major Inca rebellion against the Spanish. (The Inca national movement almost kicked the Spanish out of Peru in the 17th century.)

Contemporary research dates the festival to 1780, when, as the story goes, a young alpaca herder met a blond youth who helped him with his alpacas. According the story, his herds multiplied like crazy. The herder's father wanted to offer something back to the child, and the child asked for new clothes and offered a piece of his garment so the herder's family could match the fabric. When the father brought it to Cusco, the priest identified it as the finest canonical cloth of the Catholic Church, and another priest was sent to investigate the "sacrilege." Apparently, the child instantly disappeared into a rock, the face of Jesus appeared on the rock, the alpaca herd dropped dead from shock, and the place was considered sacred. Since then, two pilgrimages have taken place every year.

There is evidence, however, that the pilgrimages here have been going on for much longer and that the Q'uero have been attending for at least a thousand years.

Q'ollorit'i is a festival about thankfulness to Pacha Mama for all we receive from her. If you ask Don Humberto—and I did ask him—his answer is simply: "If I have a good life and I have plenty of work to buy food for my family, why would I not come to Q'ollorit'i festival to say thank you?"

Lord of Q'ollorit'i is the combination of the male power of Apu Sinak'ara (the mountain on the left side of the sanctuary); and the female power of Qolqe Punku (silver gate), the mountain range on the right side of the sanctuary if you are looking up the valley from below. From the outside, the festival resembles a mountain version of Woodstock in bad weather, minus the stage and rock bands.

People come from miles away to bring their hopes, dreams, and desires to be fulfilled by the Lord of Q'ollorit'i. An entire area is set aside for people to build doll-sized homes, right down to garages and cars in driveways. The dollhouses of the Q'ollorit'i festival have been nicknamed the magical economy on the mountain. Dreams and desires are built out of sticks into miniature towns; attendees believe if they're involved in this part of the festival they can achieve their life's goals. If you happen to walk by someone building their little house and they call to you, you *must* join them and pretend to be part of their make-believe, because you are helping to realize their goals under the eyes of the Lord of Q'ollorit'i. This area is known as the gaming area, where people play out their deepest dreams. People set up little stone enclosures made out of rocks and role-play the opening of their new business; or, if they are looking for love, they enact a mock wedding. There is even an "actor" playing the US immigration officer stamping visas for people. You play out your deepest dreams or desires and, they say, if you see Lord of Q'ollorit'i in a vision or dream, your wish will be granted. Strangely, many people dream of the same thing: to own and operate a cab company. Since many of these activities seemed strange to me, it was extremely hard to get a handle on everything.

Don Humberto no longer ventures into the crowd. He headed over to a spot on the side of the hill where there was a big boulder. This object is called the stone of Q'ueros. For him, this gathering, or at least the *intention* of this gathering, is what life is all about. It is a powerful opportunity to fulfill a great connection with Pacha Mama and to honor Lord of Q'ollorit'i. But Don is older now, and the frenetic activity in the valley is for the younger generation still trying to build their lives.

The action for the three days of this festival went something like the following. The regular people came here to pray, offer money, get blessed, and fulfill dreams. The high priests came here after a life of respecting Mother Earth and honoring Lord of Q'ollorit'i. Then there are the Ukukus. Their tradition is to arrive here and climb to the top of one of the three sacred glaciers (they are the only ones allowed to make this ascent), where they receive blessings from Lord of Q'ollorit'i and commit themselves to fighting for and protecting Mother Earth. They even carry out whipping ceremonies to show their strength and to keep themselves warm. Not too long ago, the Ukukus brought a chunk of the glacier back down with them. It was considered sacred ice, and the water could be used for blessings and healings. Global warming has stopped that practice. The Ukukus are also the police of the festival—keeping people in line and making sure everyone behaves. It's said that if you get out of line, they'll whip you.

The festival is heavy with overtones of Spanish Catholicism. During the festival, people line up by the tens of thousands and go into the church for the privilege of passing by the Jesus rock image.

The Ukukus have their own special way of paying tribute to the Jesus rock. Hundreds of groups of the Ukukus—earth warriors, each group numbering between 10 and 20—dress up and play music as they slowly parade by the rock. They dance and play with great gusto in hopes of honoring the Lord. They all play the same song, which becomes dissonant when you hear them all together at high volume. They also disguise themselves with masks and costumes, and they talk in high-pitched voices so no one will recognize them.

After the Ukukus have paraded past the Jesus rock they join the long, slow procession up the mountain to one of the sacred glaciers. Once at the top, they receive blessings and engage in competitions that see them whip each other with bullwhips—presumably to show their ability to protect Mother Earth and stay warm during the cold night. In the morning they return down to the masses, and everyone celebrates.

On the last of the three days of the festival, the archbishop of this region stands outside the church housing the Jesus rock and blesses the crowd of onlookers. The whole event is a hybrid of Catholic traditions and Incan spiritual beliefs. Yet the Andean people don't feel any contradiction. To them it is important to worship. *How* you do that is not important, so it doesn't matter what religion you follow. They don't care how you pray, just so long as you do it. They feel they are connected to a divine sacredness that goes beyond symbols.

I am not suggesting that most people here are not genuine with love in their hearts, dreams in their minds, and a real desire for spiritual uplifting and blessing. But what I was about to experience would seriously challenge my ability to give this crazy festival much credibility.

We still had one more important ceremony before Don Humberto left me to the festival. So we headed downhill and met up with my second camera crew, which had followed the people gathering from the other side. We wove our way through the crowd to climb up to a small sacred pond. This ritual was meant to be the most intense and authentic one of all: the ritual of the puka qocha, the red lake under the mountain. The lake is called Qolqe Punku, which means silver gate in Quechua, a local language. Every *karpay* (ceremony) is an initiation or transmission of the power of that place to you—the very force of nature given to the initiate. This was the meaning of our ritual at the Puka Qocha, which is the sacred lake fed by Qolqe Punku (silver gate) mountain. We were physically to bring the energy from the mountain to the rock of Jesus and the Ukukus bring the energy from Apu Sinak'ara. The whips and play and all—that's just decoration. The real deal is that you merge your energy bubble with Sinak'ara by being up there, and you bring it down to the sanctuary and tie it to the sacred stone inside. Nature needs humans to do this job—the combination of the two energies is Lord of Q'ollorit'i. My crew had set up a camp far enough from the main crowd to allow us room to pitch a number of tents and move around. The weather continued to be cold and wet, with rain turning to snow, turning to rain again. The first order of business was to get me outfitted in my Ukuku suit. Although it made me look like Bigfoot with Christmas decorations attached, it was really warm and comfortable on such a cold, damp day. Once I put on the balaclava mask, nobody knew who I was. This disguise was later to prove useful.

We started up the dirt road and into the main body of the festival. Opportunists selling trinkets of all kinds lined the road. They sold candles, snacks, supplies like lanterns and blankets, and, of course, miniature figurines for the dream houses. The most bizarre item was a donkey head (apparently for eating), which was just lying on the dirt. I don't know how old it was but it was still there three days later, when the festival ended. Price: $30.

Moving through the crowd was a brutally slow process because we were jammed shoulder to shoulder. The lone toilet facility in the middle was always packed, and it reeked and leaked. Numerous tented rooms served soups and drinks, but everything was filthy, dark, and damp. I had no interest in drinking anything that wasn't sealed let alone eating the pieces of meat hanging in the open air. And as you know, when it comes to food I'm not what anyone would call squeamish. My first impression was that this scene suggested the story of Jesus entering the temple and throwing all the money-changers' tables about and shouting at everyone to get out.

Everything Elizabeth had told me about the festival and everything I believed I would experience was about the intense spiritual energy I would be part of. She said it was something very sacred. A lot of it had to do with ancient Incan prophecies that pointed to this place and this gathering as heralding a new worldwide understanding—a shift in the greater consciousness. For Elizabeth, it seemed that even my filming could play a part in making the prophecies a reality, since my work is seen by millions of people around the world. Apparently many of the prophecies have to do with vast numbers of people and their energy combining to hit the tipping point of a greater consciousness. It was all highly metaphysical. But when I first saw all the blue tarps and then began to walk among the "money-changers," I could feel my hopes of an authentic spiritual experience turning to disillusionment.

My Q'uero interpreter, Fredy, led me to the group of Ukukus I was to join. The Ukukus are all men under 30, since the festival is meant to be a place where they prove their bravery and strength to be worthy of protecting Pacha Mama. They are also committing service to their communities. They were really nice men and welcomed us warmly. Fredy, a local Andean, was also thrilled to become an honorary Ukuku for the night. He had been to the festival before, but had never been an Ukuku.

Each Ukuku group had its own area where it would practice its singing and dancing for the Jesus rock. It looked like some kind of high school rally with all sorts of teams and bands, along with banners and colors.

My Ukuku group and I joined the long procession slowly making its way into the church. Only after we presented ourselves to the Jesus rock could we begin our trek up the mountain to take part in what I like to call the Ukuku games. While waiting outside the church, I took my mask off to cool down for a bit. Suddenly I heard someone say behind me, "Hey, Surbiberman!" in broken English. I was recognized by a South American fan of my other TV series, *Survivorman*—the last thing I wanted.

Then I was grabbed from behind. I'm not a violent guy, but my old reflexes kicked in and I just about turned to clobber the dude and send him back where he came from. But when I turned, I saw that he was drunk. This was a bit of a turning point for me: a drunk? I thought this was a place of worship and energy and reverence for Mother Earth. How could there be a drunk here? But I started to notice more drunks; after all, this was a festival for young people. Sometime later, the Ukukus were alerted to this man's drunken behavior. He was then held down and whipped. There were rumblings of real police—if they ever decide to come here—stopping that kind of activity. For now, the Ukukus handle it on their own.

It was close to midnight when we finally entered the church. As we drew closer to the entrance, our leader instructed us to start our dance and to really ramp it up. The members of my group showed me the dance while in the lineup to the church. Fortunately I'm a quick learner when it comes to dance moves, so I just followed along. We couldn't forget the steps, and we had to be exuberant. After all, Jesus was watching.

The weird part of all this was that I had a video camera on a tripod. I also had camera operators in the church waiting to film me, and they didn't know what I looked like in the sea of mask-wearing Ukukus. All around us, the festival exploded in colors, sights, and sounds: dancing, music, fireworks, high-pitched voices, whippings, and praying. I wasn't sure what to expect when I got inside the church. Was I going to see the image of Jesus and be overwhelmed? Was I going to have a spiritual epiphany? How intense was this going to be? Or was I going to become cynical and skeptical and see only heavy Catholic symbolism with its candles, neon lights, robes, and rituals?

I wasn't even sure where to look as I passed the barricade that separated the Jesus rock from the main part of the church. We were each given only a second or two, just enough time to walk by. I glanced to my right to see the image. There was a big glass wall in front, adorned with plants and crosses and colored material. Behind it all was a wall of rock decorated with all these things and a portrait of Jesus in the recognizable position on the cross . . . painted on the rock. And that was it: a gold-and-black painted Jesus. I walked out the back door with my group of spiritual warriors, mask in hand. (You can't wear a mask in the church.)

We finally found our way to an area in the crowd—about 25 by 60 feet—where we were to perform our dance and have our whipping competitions. There were even supposed to be judges milling about, confirming the group had done a good job, but I never did see any. I also became confused because I thought the whipping was reserved for the top of the glacier, and we hadn't even started that trek yet. All around us were tens of thousands of people. Fireworks exploded throughout the festival every 20 seconds. And that song was maddening: the same melody over and over again, sung by hundreds of different groups. You couldn't escape its shrill call.

Once we completed doing our dances for the crowd, we got into the whipping competition, where two men square off against each other using bullwhips. Though the whips can do some serious damage to your body, you don't really feel them if you're padded. The competition is essentially a test of pain tolerance: the two men stand a foot or two apart and whip each other's calves. If you want to up the ante, you lift your costume so that you're more exposed on the calves. There's also a referee who can step in and stop the competition when it goes on for too long or gets out of hand.

My spirit of competition once again welled up inside me, and I jumped in the ring to kick some Ukuku ass. Neither I nor my opponent held back, so I think we proved our worth as good warriors. But there's more. Once everyone has had their fight, they run the gauntlet of their group and get whipped at their legs as they run, jump, or walk on by. Most run. The tougher ones walk, acting all the while like it doesn't hurt. It doesn't, really. Well, okay, it sort of does. As I said, I was in a competitive mood so I lifted up my pant legs to expose my calves and then walked slowly through the gauntlet, being whipped by a dozen men without flinching. It all sounds dark and strange, yet at this point it plays out a lot more like a carnival. But a carnival wasn't what I was here for.

With the dancing and whipping and meetin' Jesus all done, it was time for something a little tougher: the long climb up the mountain with a few thousand other Ukukus. All the groups must go up en masse. You must stay together and not lose your place in line. At this point it was nearing about one in the morning. It was dark, cold and damp.

On the way to the base of the glacier, we had to walk through the massive crowd. Once through it, we then had to navigate the secondary area that hundreds of the people used as the bathroom. This section was right out in the open, and there were feces everywhere. It was, in a word, disgusting. At this point I was beginning to think, "I don't care how spiritual or religious this is. Where is the respect for Pacha Mama in all this?"

I had just spent a week with an Incan spiritual elder experiencing ceremony after ceremony while climbing the mountains, in preparation for becoming an official Ukuku, but nothing here seemed right. I may not be Andean, but I'm no fool. And this was beginning to look like a ridiculous gathering of young adults playing out religious rituals. As I said before, I'm sure that most people here had good intentions, but there was a darker underbelly to all this. I was beginning to worry about sharing my feelings with my hosts Elizabeth and Fredy; the experience with the drunk didn't help.

We gathered at the foot of the trail to the glacier, this time with Andrew and Johnny at my side. We had been assured that we could all go up and film the time on the glacier. Both my cameramen had to wear Ukuku costumes, but Andrew looked horribly out of place. I'm five-foot-nine and I already looked tall among these people. At six-foot-four, Andrew had zero chance of concealing his identity. Throw in the camera on his shoulder and we were anything but inconspicuous.

The trail up the mountain was wide enough for only one person. Standing there, blocking the entrance was a guy who was obviously in charge. He motioned that we wouldn't be allowed to go up. I gasped. This climb would be hugely significant to my filming. As with most of my trips, I didn't leave home until I had absolutes about what I needed to film and where I could go. To be refused the journey up the mountain would jeopardize the entire production. This last leg of the journey was the whole point of the show and my journey! Thankfully, Fredy stepped in and worked his diplomatic magic, and we started the trudge uphill. But our troubles were far from over.

The walk was slow but steep and relentless. Within a hundred yards and a few minutes, we were panting heavily with our lower-elevation–conditioned lungs. The climb, which would never be anything other than very steep, would take at least six hours. Andrew, 24 years old and fit, was pretty good with it all. Johnny and I, on the other hand, were about to face one hell of a physical challenge. As we slowly put one leg in front of the other, the Andean men joked, skipped, laughed, danced, talked nonstop in their annoying faked high-pitched voices, and continually played that same damn song on their flutes while climbing!

Though we stopped as a group only twice on the entire journey, both stops were long enough for us to get a serious chill on. We were sweaty from the climb, and the long waits were hypothermia-inducing. Someone once said, "You sweat, you die!"

At the first stop Johnny sat with Andrew and me and said, "Sorry, guys, I can't do this. I can't make it." Johnny's a tough guy, so it was saying a lot that he couldn't manage the rest of the climb. The funny part was he now had to spend the next few hours going back down the one-person path against the tide of humanity making its way up to the glacier.

Andrew, Fredy, and I continued up the hill with our group of Ukukus like some kind of chain gang, every one of us wearing comical puffy suits made of alpaca fur. My legs were burning and my lungs about to burst. We were at 17,000 feet and the climb was relentless. Yet the Andean men skipped up like they were walking on a flat road at sea level.

Things got weird at our second stop. All the groups gathered in a circle of rocks. It was now about 4 a.m., and I was exhausted and just wanted to sleep. But I also wanted to get on with it and see what all the fuss was about on the glacier. We were almost there. That's when I noticed we had somehow lost track of our own group of Ukukus. It was just me, Andrew, Fredy and a group of Ukukus we didn't recognize. We sat for at least an hour with nothing happening. Everyone was getting badly chilled. Little candle fires were burning and guys held their hands over the flames in the mountain night wind. We were nearly at the top of the mountain, and it was dark and cold. There was nowhere flat to sit, only frosted, jagged rocks. I tried to sleep in a twisted position, but it was impossible. In all my years as Survivorman I hadn't experienced a worse place to sleep.

Then some men of authority started talking, and talking, and talking. Of course it was all in Spanish, so I didn't understand a word. All the while the young Ukukus were talking in their high-pitched voices, giggling and telling jokes. But you could see that people were mad.

Ultimately it became a frustrating, boring, endless discussion about how no one is respecting the customs properly any longer, so no one was going to be allowed to go up. Well, no one except all the people the authority figures deemed okay to go. So they began a long, drawn-out process of choosing the groups that could go up. But before that could happen, a member of each group was allowed to make his case. These are Spanish people, and they can talk! Hours of bone-chilling boredom sitting on frozen jagged rocks passed by. Finally the leaders read the list of the groups that were allowed to go. One by one the groups got up and left for the glacier. I hadn't understood a word of the entire process but I grasped one thing: when they were finished listing all the groups and everyone had left, the only people left sitting there, out of more than a hundred Ukukus, were Fredy, Andrew, me, and six drunken kids.

Fredy was our link to everything. He spoke the language and knew the customs. He, too, had donned an Ukuku suit for the night and I had been sticking to him like glue for fear of losing him. It was bad enough we had lost track of our Ukuku group, but now something was really wrong. Hours and hours of climbing, one gasping step at a time, brought us to the main event, the most sacred of places, the glacier itself, the place where we commune with Lord of Q'ollorit'i, the spirit of the mountain. We were so close.

With all the other groups headed up the hill, I turned to Fredy and said, "Let's just go last in line. They'll never notice us tagging along at the end." It worked for about a hundred yards. Then a big guy came back with three escorts playing the tough card and told us to stop. Fredy went into his magic diplomacy routine, but this time it didn't work. In fact, they turned on him and said he was not an offi-cial tour guide from the city and it was illegal for him to guide Andrew and me up the mountain. This comment was preposterous, of course, because such a situation didn't even exist.

Fredy played their game, however, and told them he just didn't have his card on him (not true). That wasn't good enough, though, and with their chests all puffed out, they refused to let these two white guys step on the glacier. I was livid, but not surprised. What a hell of a journey to undertake, only to be denied entrance mere feet from the finish line. All the while we had been secretly filming the big blowhard with his grand posturing, by holding small cameras at our waistlines and pointing them up at him. So I got an idea and had Andrew pull his camera out to have me speak to the camera right there on the mountainside. That's when the big guy, who as it turned out was the mayor of his town, came back down the hill singing a completely different tune. Through Fredy, he asked us to answer one simple question: "Do you vouch for Fredy as being a real guide?" But he wasn't looking at us; he was looking at the camera. Of course, I said yes. And with that, he stretched out his arms and gave me a big hug to welcome me in the name of Q'ollorit'i.

Afterward Fredy said it was because of the cameras. The blowhard just wanted to be on film. It makes sense. It was the weirdest about-face I had ever seen for someone given a chance to be on TV. He even helped me keep going by offering me coca leaves and rubbing my face with his hands and a splash of sacred water he had in a bottle, since I was short of breath this high up the mountain.

We had been climbing as Ukukus all through the night. Now that daylight was dawning, I was glad to be moving again since the time sitting among the rocks was pure torture. We continued to climb, this time up the snow and ice. If we slipped and fell it would be a long fall, and most likely fatal.

As we stepped onto the glacier, it became clear that each of the hundred or so groups had its own way of celebrating up here. Some were somber. Some were boisterous. We could see the other groups on the other glaciers close by. By the time we got to the top area, the gathering was about a hundred people or so, most of them about the age of 25, and Fredy told me they were from the same town. We were clustered in the outline of a rectangular shape of people about 40 feet across at the bottom and a hundred feet long leading up to the top, where the action was. And what was this action anyway? I couldn't even see what was happening. Fredy explained that, if we wanted to, we could follow to the top. It wasn't mandatory. And up there we would receive a sort of baptism.

Slowly we ascended the slippery slope of snow, never standing but using our hands to climb. When people were finished doing whatever it was they did up there, they slid back down through the crowd toboggan-style to great cheers while everyone threw snowballs at them. As I reached the top I caught

a glimpse of the action. First I was to bow to the cross, then kiss a whip, then bend over while some dude (he was not a church official, I can tell you that much) whipped my ass while I looked at the cross, then kiss the whip again, then slide down the snowball lane. One man was doing all the whipping, but, as my turn came, the mayor himself, with a smile of delight, took the whip and personally whipped my ass three times—hard; very hard; a whipping for my sins. I kissed the whip and slid down the hill to cheers of delight, apparently baptized.

Perhaps I was just stuck in my own skepticism. Fredy wasn't fazed by any of the contradictions. He loved it all and vowed to come back and do the climb again. Maybe I was just too tired. But none of this left me with a good feeling. I failed to make the connection between all this over-the-top Spanish Catholicism hybrid and what it meant in terms of reconnecting with Mother Earth.

My heart ached to see Don Humberto again for reassurance; to once again feel the gentle, humble, yet powerful energy of his presence and understanding. Did I feel a powerful connection to Mother Earth, and did I feel reconnected to the earth after all these years? Absolutely. Then what does it mean now? Where does all this symbolism and religious crap meet up with a greater consciousness and protecting the earth for all time?

I looked inside my mind and my heart and then stood quietly up there on the glacier. Amid the high-pitched chatter and giggles, my feet freezing in the snow and ice, the sound of the whip in the air, and the view down below to some kind of religious rock concert, I decided to tap into that voice again: the voice I had heard at the sacred Incan site with Kucho during the San Pedro ceremony, the voice of Mother Earth. The response was immediate and clear as a bell: "It's not about numbers, Les. It never has been. It is about intention."

And that was it. Nothing more. Respecting the earth and connecting to God is not a game of numbers. Spiritual revelation. Quantum physics. Metaphysics. Scientific research and analysis. Meditative states. Earth medicines that serve as portals. The Secret. In the end, all of it comes down to *intention*. When we let the universe know our intentions, it responds and we create our world. Prophecies notwithstanding, we continue to create who we are and what will befall us, good, bad, or indifferent.

The road to hell is *not* paved with good intentions. That's a lie.

13

SINGING SHAMAN SONGS

The Mentawai

It had been a year of preparation, the struggle through the process, and then, finally, the revelation. But my last experience had tainted me. It was indeed a reality check. If I had become too caught up in the metaphysics of it all with my experience in plant medicines and the Incan high priests, then the Q'ollorit'i festival served to bring me back to my skeptical self. But I no longer questioned why I was here, and that in itself was a profound change for me.

I try hard to balance out the issues. My mind meticulously dissects the questions at hand and I sit there with all the options on the table, willing to give each one of them a fair shake. Don't ever try to debate a topic with me; I will frustrate the hell out of you in my Libra way.

So when I boarded the plane to Sumatra, an island in western Indonesia and the last shoot of the series, I wasn't looking for any more spiritual development or revelations. The Q'ollorit'i festival had worn me out. I went to Sumatra only to shoot the survival stuff and get tattooed in their traditional ways, with a rusty nail and a stick. I had no intention of learning anything else spiritually, metaphysically, psychologically, or any other kind of "ically." I should have known better.

Departing from the port of Padang, Indonesia, in two boats, we had to cross an area of ocean known for pirates. My crew this time was Johnny, Peter, Andrew, and Laura, along with our connection and interpreter to the Mentawai, Charlie Lambe.

The coastal village of Muara Siberut, off the southeast coast of the island of Siberut, is a filthy and polluted little place on the edge of the ocean. One could easily walk around the village on the cement sidewalk that snakes along above the little drainage ditches full of garbage and dead fish. Under the intensely hot tropical sun, it smelled . . . bad. Piled remains of burned garbage—food and all—were strewn on the sidewalk in front of each house. Much of it was only half-burned thanks to the frequent heavy rains, so the garbage would fall into the filthy little canal and eventually make its way out into the ocean a few hundred yards away.

The Mentawai, who are only a day's dugout canoe ride up a shallow little river from Muara Siberut, are a remote tribe whose people are still considered savages by the villagers living at the mouth of the river on the coast (even though many of those more "civilized" villagers are descendants of the Mentawai themselves).

NEARLY ALL THE REMOTE PEOPLES I have lived with, survived with, and performed ceremonies with over the previous year existed only a stone's throw from civilization, so assimilation seems so much like just a matter of time. The one exception are the Hewa of Papua New Guinea, but even they were facing a massive mine project that saw researchers visit their remote jungle village. I know still uncontacted tribes are hidden in the Amazon jungle, but I fear the romantic image of the unaffected remote culture is today all but gone on this planet.

So it becomes a matter of asking whether these remote peoples can keep their culture, while under the influence of the outside world. I'm not saying we should put them in a big glass bubble and study them like a grade school science project. But "teaching them better ways" or trying to "civilize" them is a pretty arrogant way for outsiders to think. I return to my vision of the cultural triangle: spirituality, land skills, and language. Keeping them in loincloths and chanting around a fire seems a little clichéd.

An older Waorani man from the Ecuadorian Amazon once asked me, "Do you live like your grandfather did?" "No," I answered. "Then why do you want me to live like mine?" he continued. He had a good point.

Though living on opposite sides of the globe, the Hewa and the Inuit seem to share something. They are adopting methods of modern technology, but still love the land. Perhaps more important, they still love their connection to the land. Is that it? Is that perhaps the greatest and most profound potential loss when we assimilate a remote culture into our own? Simply not loving the land anymore? These Mentawai were about to teach me a lesson in connectedness to the earth.

We needed at least 12 dugout canoes propelled by motors called pom poms (named for the sound they make) to take all our gear. Just as we were leaving the village, the off-and-on jungle rains began. It was hard to decide which to prefer, the heavy rains or the beating hot tropical sun.

Tarocha was his name. In this grouping of houses in the jungle (a house here is called an Uma), he was the head shaman. He was an older man, wiry and lean, with skin as leathery as you might imagine a jungle native's to be. But he had a permanent smile as he greeted me with much enthusiasm and a handshake.

We were not the first to visit Tarocha and his clan. Charlie Lambe, our guide, had once brought in a photographer who was doing a study on tattooing around the world. He has also brought in the occasional anthropologist or group of interested people. But I was the first outsider who was asking to share in the Mentawai lifestyle and live as the locals do, even to the point of heading out on a monkey hunt with them deep into the jungle. This approach made Tarocha very happy. These are a welcoming people. They know outsiders mean supplies, and frankly, as it would be anywhere else for people who live in isolation, our presence meant company and a break from the monotony of jungle existence.

TOO OFTEN WE FORGET THAT PEOPLE ARE PEOPLE. Every remote living culture I have had the pleasure of surviving with experiences jealousy, love, hate, arguments, theft, forgiveness, playfulness, and the gamut of other human emotions and qualities we all deal with daily. This is why I try to take everyone at face value. You never know what you are going to get. I have had good experiences and bad experiences with people no matter how they live or what they know about the world. I don't over-romanticize remote cultures. It was always a debate between Laura and me. For her, the remote cultures seemed more beautiful than our own, their spirituality more spiritual, their deepness more deep, and their hearts more profound. But I have seen remote people lie, cheat, and steal. And I have seen born-and-bred New Yorkers show compassion and love as deep as the ocean. People are people, no matter where we live. All that said, the Mentawai are a cheerful, accepting people from the get-go, at least to outsiders.

The Mentawai are true animists. They believe that *everything* that exists has a soul, not just humans and plants and animals, but also the rocks and water. God is everywhere. Quantum physics: this "unknown force within all things" seems to be a recurring theme resonating throughout all my life's experiences. Harmony between one's soul and the natural earth is a guiding principle in the lives of the Mentawai, too. And so it should be in ours, before it is too late and we find that we have destroyed the very earth we depend on for our existence. So before cutting or killing or capturing anything, permission must be asked and gratitude offered.

I headed into the jungle with Tarocha. With him were Amanipa and Jacobus. Amanipa, who represented the younger generation, was also the best hunter in the jungle. Jacobus, a generation younger than Amanipa, represented the hope that the tradition of shamanism and jungle life would continue. The next few days played out like so many others that I have experienced on my journeys. We hunted together and survived out in the jungle without the benefit of speaking each other's language. We laughed and joked and seriously hunted, hoping not to come back empty-handed—a result that's too often the norm in a territory shrunken by the encroachment of the outside world. Even so, the government has set aside large tracts of land as jungle reserves and forbidden the Mentawai from hunting in those areas. No consideration was given to the remote jungle tribes; they were simply informed that they could no longer hunt in areas that once sustained them.

We split into two groups: Tarocha and me; and the other two younger men off on their own. With the jungle rain coming down hard all night and all day, Tarocha and I found ourselves waiting it out under a little shelter. We were careful not to let the leeches burrow into our skin, which they can do so quickly, while we tended a little smoky fire under the palm leaves. Even with the pouring rain it was still hot enough to sit nearly naked, which this time I didn't do because the leeches have a nasty habit of trying to go up a man's urethra. (It makes me wince even thinking about it today.)

That's when Tarocha made something clear to me that caught me off guard. He considered me to be a visiting shaman. He began to sing and, as he sang, harmonized with the natural world and the spirits around him. For a shaman, this is the goal of singing: to harmonize in the purest sense of the word with the spirit world. He never once assumed that he had anything to teach me. He wasn't going to prepare me or protect me for any great journey. He looked at me and simply decided that I was a visiting shaman and gave me a name that meant "he who is very busy." In their culture, visiting shamans harmonize by teaching each other shaman songs. It shows respect and is vital to the relationship. So he asked me to show him my songs. With a few thousand under my belt from a life as a songwriter, it was no problem. I taught him the melody to my song "Long Walk Home," and he followed me in the tune.

Of course, I am not a shaman. At least I have not ever been officially trained by anyone or any tribe to be one. I can't heal anyone, or I haven't learned to heal. I don't have visions, and I can't see spirits. I don't have any psychic abilities, and so far God hasn't revealed any master plan to me. I'm just a filmmaker and musician, someone who loves all things wild and free. But with the acceptance by Tarocha I felt like I had arrived, like that arbitrary scheduling of ceremonies originally based on nothing more than logistics had ended up following some kind of predetermined year-long vision quest for me. It was as if nothing had happened to me by chance. First the preparation and protection. Then the process. Then the breakthroughs. Then the reality of it all. And finally acceptance.

Tarocha was reading me. What did he see? Had my experiences of this past year brought me to a new place of understanding that was visible to someone who was so in touch with the energy of the earth? Tarocha lived every moment of his life connecting with nature and honoring and respecting everything, from rocks to trees to insects and mammals. This connectedness to the planet has been a thread through all my experiences, not only from this past year of filming, but throughout my whole life, whether I was aware of it or not.

When we returned from the jungle, there were two things left to do with Tarocha. The first was to dance, possibly to a state of trance, with a couple of other visiting shamans. Because I was a visiting shaman, they assumed, I would join them and dance with them. The second was to get a traditional tattoo, the mark of a shaman. Only shamans are usually permitted to get the traditional tattoos.

The inclination of an outsider is to question what all the tattooing means, so I asked. The images didn't really mean anything he said. They are simply a way to make the body more beautiful. But this is where the depth comes in. Listen to Tarocha's explanation: The shamans try to make their bodies look more beautiful by teeth-filing, tattooing, plucking eyebrows, and wearing flowers so that the good spirit which lives within them will want to stay. Simple and deep: treat your body well and try to make it beautiful, for it is the temple of the spirit.

In a shaman's life, the tattooing starts on the front of each shoulder in the form of the sun. These tattoos represent the story of how the sun got into the sky. At one time the sun was too close to the earth, so the hunters got together and shot their arrows at it to push it back farther up into the sky and to not be so hot.

The tattoos then flow down the body, a new one every now and again until one day, likely into the ripe old age of 40, they finish off with tattoo ankle bracelets. The whole process is an organic and beautiful thing for this group of animists. The tricky part is *how* they do it. I'm not talking sanitary Western tattoo parlor here. To the contrary, they tap them into your skin with a small and sometimes rusty nail. This process is actually far less painful than the teeth-chiseling the Mentawai women often endure, but either way I knew I was about to have an elderly jungle shaman tap a nail into my skin for a couple of hours.

The ink is derived from a mixture of soot from the bottom of a cooking pot and sugar cane juice. The tools are finely crafted pieces of wood, one with a small nail embedded in one end. As they began the process, tapping into my skin just above my pre-existing North American tattoo of a wolf, I lay back with some trepidation, but was pleasantly surprised to find that it didn't hurt too much. In fact, I would say there were spots that a New York tattoo artist hit a year before which were even more painful. But when it came to the second tattoo, something wasn't working. The younger shaman spent an hour over top of me only to discover that he hadn't really put enough ink on the nail. So now the older shaman (with bad eyesight) took over tapping the nail with thicker ink, back into all the previous holes.

The sweat started to drip down my face in the intense tropical jungle heat. The elderly Mentawai women hovered over my shoulders, shouting out directions to the shamans and arguing with them, I suppose about technique and design. Their banana leaf cigarettes hung perpetually from their lips; they looked like truckers. Then, out of nowhere, I felt the strangest sensation. That's when I noticed that the old lady hovering behind my back was reaching over in absolute laughing hysterics, tweaking my nipples and pulling at the hair on my chest. It provided entertainment for them for an hour while the old shaman just kept tapping a nail into my blackened, ink- and blood-stained skin.

The risk of infection in the jungle is high, so immediately after finishing the second tattoo they took me down to a nearby stream to wash me off and aggressively rub medicinal plants into the tattoo wounds. I think this was the most painful part of the day, but we finished up with many smiles and the Mentawai men even took turns flexing their featherweight, boxer-like muscles with me to great laughter.

The day finished with all of us gathering and eating the jungle pig they had been boiling for many hours. It tasted disgusting, but I ate right along with them out of respect and to honor their hospitality. The intestines and hearts of pigs and chickens are pulled out and saved for reading the signs. The men told me that, in the heart of the pig, they can read about my visit, and they took it as a good omen about my intentions for being here. Just by interpreting the lines and the markings of blood and veins, they formed their shamanic opinions about what has been happening now and what is going to happen in the future. No different from "reading the bones" or tarot cards.

Late that night we gathered with the visiting shamans and prepared ourselves for trance dancing and reading the intestines. The outside of the Uma (house) was decorated as if for a wedding, with tall poles erected and palm leaves split and woven onto them. Inside, everyone was decorating their bodies. The women got into the action, too, applying face paint, colored feathers, painted leaves, headdresses, and beads.

Our dances represented animal spirits. The shamans attempted to be overcome and possessed by the spirits of birds and mammals. Only one of them went the full way, though, bringing himself to the point of shaking, trembling, and falling into exhaustion on the floor of the wooden Uma. He said he was struck by the vision of a spirit dancing beside him and was simply overwhelmed.

We chased bad spirits out of the building using branches and leaves, effectively "sweeping" them out. We rang bells, chanted, and sang to welcome the good spirits. A rooster was sacrificed, and the shaman read more intestines. We danced, imitating the movements of monkeys, birds, and wild cats to connect with the spirits through mimicry. But this time I wasn't worried about being able to trance. It's not my place. I took it all in stride and eventually retired to the sidelines to let them finish out the dance.

These Mentawai are about as primitive as it gets on this planet, and in their *lack* of progress they have retained a connection to the natural world that my own culture seems to have lost. They retain a balance and harmony with the earth that I can only envy—a balance and harmony that we as a "civilized" society should be embracing.

Before it's too late.

The Mentawai, like so many remote tribes, allow semi-domesticated pigs to roam the jungle. The pigs grow, get fat, and then are hunted when necessary, bypassing all the effort of farming the pigs in pens and eliminating the associated costs. But jungle life for the pigs is not fun, and they're even filthier and nastier tempered than farmed pigs. The pigs for our feast had been caught and trapped in pens deep in the jungle. Just getting hold of them in their little bamboo-pole enclosures was a brutal task—we held them down with our feet and hands and all our body weight and tied them up as tightly as possible, all the while trying to stay out of range of their teeth. One bite from these pigs would have been extremely dangerous out in the jungle.

After an hour of tangling with the beasts, all of us—five grown men, including me—were exhausted and filthy. And the pigs still needed to be carried miles through the jungle. On our backs. On my back! And this pig, now tied tightly in a wicker basket and firmly pressed against my back, is crawling with fleas and parasites. Did I mention that I am carrying it on my back? For miles. Through a hot and wet jungle. For miles. On my back.

Yeah, let's not even go there. I prefer to not think about it too much or I start itching. Good thing I like bacon.

EPILOGUE

As a young boy I played outside my cottage in the forest, pretending to survive. I made pillows out of moss and put branches up for crude shelter roofs. I talked to trees and bugs and animals. It was my escape. My refuge from a mediocre life in suburbia. I dreamed of being like Jacques Cousteau. I dreamed of being like Tarzan. And, lo and behold: what is Survivorman if not the perfect hybrid of those two dreams? But in the adult world of television production, my reason for those dreams—connecting to nature—disappeared into the din of business, money, and schedules.

The year-long vision quest as I now know it to be, while creating the series *Beyond Survival,* served to reconnect me. I remember now to walk barefoot in the forest. I remember now to commune with nature and spend free time in the beauty that is the wild world. I remember always to stop and drink from a fresh running stream in my own little tradition to connect me to the spirit of the land I am walking on. The next mission of my life has become solidified with the knowledge that we as a society need to reconnect with nature. How can we love and respect and care for it if we do not know it? How can we even begin to know it if we never experience it?

We can play soccer, but it doesn't give us a chance to really smell the grass and touch the earth. We can play hockey, but it doesn't give us a chance to taste and feel the snow. All of my life I have enjoyed active physical pursuits without coming anywhere close to being an athlete. I have loved organized sports, and I love it in the lives of my kids. But there is no replacement for smelling the grass, touching the earth, tasting and feeling the snow. Essentially, free time in nature. Walking barefoot on the earth will do more to activate your personal energies than anything that requires cleats. Splashing in a fresh lake or river will do more to awaken your senses than any video game challenge. These outdoor pursuits are the actions that involve every single sense you have. We all come alive when we get outdoors because our dormant "natural intelligence," our inborn skill set of connecting to nature, is set free once again. Just breathing in deeply in a field, or "forest bathing" as the Japanese call it, will stimulate your brain so much that you begin to physically heal, emotionally heal, and spiritually come alive. And these are not hypothetical, philosophical, hopeful meandering thoughts of mine. This is now actual, proven science.

Our indoor, plugged-in activities set us on a path of dull expressions, listlessness, and apathy. Our blood pools in our legs and butts. Our eyes weaken. Our muscles atrophy. Okay—so now we have highly advanced hand–eye coordination. Well, doesn't that sound profound for the soul? I don't think so! Paddle a canoe, and you become more alive and able to handle stress. Walk in the forest, and you acquire stronger character and are able to love better. Sit in a field, and you become more intelligent. Dangle your feet in a stream, and you heal more quickly. Climb a mountain, and you build muscles in every part of your body.

This bears repeating: there is *no* substitute for free time in natural surroundings. And the best part is this: you don't have to go to the jungle or a desert. You don't have to fly to Africa or Peru. You don't have to arrange lengthy time off work to make a big trip happen. You have creeks and small forests and parks close to you, from Central Park, New York, to some field behind a hospital. Take a walk. Walk your dog there. Walk your neighbor's dog there. But one way or another, get down to the place that has falling leaves, tall grass, bird nests, buzzing bees, fluttering butterflies, moss-covered rocks, and tangled vines. Now just breathe. Or just sit. Or climb. Or walk. Or swim. Or dig. Or watch. Or smell. Or . . .

If we envision a world with flourishing ecosystems and cultural diversity, then we shall have these things. It truly is our universe to create. I have traveled to the remote, supposedly "pristine" corners of the earth and found plastic floating in the water. But I have also flown all day over jungles and landed in areas where there are still undiscovered species of wildlife. So I have hope.

The efforts of North American governments to be environmentally responsible bring long-overdue regulations to the general population, but miss the big beast of industry. Industry and corporate interests still win the day, to the detriment of the planet itself. Corporate ego runs rampant and in favor of short- and long-term profit for owners before all other concerns. Incredibly shortsighted and immature perspectives such as destroying expansive pristine habitats in favor of farming or mining, while believing that it will all "just grow back," still exist. Unfortunately, they exist within circles of power and influence.

More than 70 million sharks are taken from the ocean each year; scientists say their population has been reduced by 98 percent. Shark finning is one of the main reasons. It's a practice through which sharks are caught, have their fins cut off, and are then thrown back into the ocean, still alive, to sink to the bottom and die an agonizing death. The initiative of banning shark fins in some cities has been successful but not before hearing from a large contingent of the Chinese community. One of the speakers, sharing a perspective accepted by their group at large, stated that all sharks should be wiped out of the ocean to the point of extinction so that "the other species would have a chance to live and be fished." Unbelievable opinions like this one are why, because of the voraciousness of Asian fishing fleets, tuna stocks are getting smaller and smaller. Dolphins, too, are slaughtered by the thousands, often during the process of finding "clean" specimens to imprison in zoo-type aquariums. Now manta rays and sea cucumbers (a species responsible for the health of coral reefs) are under attack, as is just about anything else the long-liner boats can rip out of the waters. Local third world fishermen are offered a year's wages for a week's work to harvest whatever the Japanese or Thai fishing boats ask of them. This type of arrangement wiped out massive coral reefs in the area of Tonga. Soon the oceans may be home to little more than jellyfish and fish farms. The sea then becomes one giant farm.

But there comes a small moment in time when the tipping point toward a new reality is reached. And when that happens, things can change . . . for the better. So what should the healthy continuation of our species on this planet look like? What will it take to tip the planet back before it's too late? One person. It starts in the form of one person making a change and adjusting his or her very own life to seek to live in harmony with the planet. The simple energy of one person is enough to change the entire planet. But I fear that now it may be too little, too late. Blue boxes and recycling your tin and glass are quaint efforts that make you feel good. Don't stop. But it's not enough to save the planet.

We live in an age where each person must learn to work with others until the combined positive energy overrides the destruction and downward-spiraling path the health of our planet has taken. Each environmental faction, group, agency, society, and organization must combine and galvanize efforts. A few solid and unified voices will be more effective than hundreds of small voices trying to be heard by government. Divided we fall. And so will the planet with us. United we can reverse the looming destruction of our healthy planet.

The spectrum of concerned organizations and individuals is wide. From aggressive eco-saboteurs like Paul Watson and his Sea Shepherd organization, ramming and sinking Japanese whaling boats; to learned scientists like David Suzuki articulating what we all need to hear through media and keynotes; to children in classrooms recycling everything they get their hands on and cleaning up local natural areas—our efforts should remain wide, but ultimately become united under one common goal.

The revolution that will come from today's children will be an environmental one. We should not be waiting for them to revolt. The change must come *now* so that they don't have to. When the greater consciousness of individuals outnumbered the supporters of slavery, it was abolished. The beliefs of greed and environmental destruction must share the same fate as slavery. Shift your energy now toward securing the future of cultural diversity and the health of the physical manifestation of Mother Earth.

If you don't take a stance now, I believe the younger generation will have to take one later. First by revolt, then, sadly, by war. Today's terrorism will be forgotten as a series of isolated, religiously motivated occurrences. The big war will be based on the environment. Ironically, the environment will suffer the hardest blow when that happens.

There are a hundred things we can do in our daily lives. We hear about them in the news all the time. I used to scoff a little at what I thought was a quaint phrase: "Think globally, act locally." I am humbler now. For it is still the answer. I know this statement sounds like I'm bragging, but I don't have garbage anymore. I simply stopped producing it. There is a place for everything I discard, from soiled wrappers and broken glass to filthy rags and busted bikes. I frustrate my guests with the fact that there is no garbage receptacle in my house. It's not easy, and I am often frustrated as I try to figure out how not to throw something into the garbage. Just what *do* you do with dental floss anyway? There are details to work out. Your area may not have the infrastructure in place. But, if you care, it is doable.

As far as I'm concerned, garbage should be illegal. So close off your garbage container for one month and see how it all becomes possible. Create the universe our own species needs to flourish, one with a sea of green roofs over every industrial building in existence, one with all other species intact, and one with cultural diversity that does not prey on the destruction of the environment, wildlife, or other humans.

We don't have to resign ourselves to the fact that we are simply going to hell in a handbasket. We don't need to give up and just enjoy what we have while we have it. Getting the giants of industry to volunteer is not enough. Laws need to be made. Budgets need to be diverted. It is an incredibly small world. What someone does in Siberia will affect someone in Chile; what someone does in Malaysia will affect someone in Wyoming. We are all connected. A tree breathes out and we breathe in, we breathe out and a tree breathes in. *How much more connected to the natural world can you be?* The lyrics of that traditional spiritual "He's Got the Whole World in His Hands" should be changed to "*We've* got the whole world in *our* hands." God is not going to sweep down from the sky and clean up the oceans, bring back the whales, and freshen the air. We continue to create our own universe.

What are *you* creating?

NUMBERS CRUNCHED

Miles traveled—over 300,000

Meals on a plane—187

Movies watched in flight—72

Delays (in hours)—143

Bags lost—0

Bags delayed in flight—16

Hours in flight—please don't remind us

Bags stolen—1 (Laura's)

Months' worth of nights in hotel rooms—24

Coffees consumed—3,423 (3,013 by Laura)

Hours in airports—OMG!

Cases of malaria—2

Cases of dysentry—32

Romances started—1

Sunrises filmed—117

Sunsets filmed—157

PLACES VISITED

Ontario	Namibia
Baffin Island (Pond Inlet)	Botswana
British Columbia	Fiji
Alaska	Bahamas
Georgia	Cayman Islands
Arizona	Madagascar
California	Grenada
Peru	Argentina
Ecuador	Papua New Guinea
Costa Rica	Indonesia
Mexico	Sri Lanka
Belize	Colorado
Florida	Norway
South Africa	Malaysia
Cook Islands	Borneo
Australia	Sumatra

"One Giant Farm"

You hunt the dolphins, kill the whales

And bloodstains drip from your sails

Farm the forests, farm the seas

Long-line and strip mine with ease

Corporate farming, corporate mines

Will nothing be left behind?

I know this world is smaller now

Don't ignore this simple truth

The earth is not one giant farm

Tell me where now can I roam, I roam

Tell me where now is my home, my wilderness home

Tell me where now I can go to hear the song of the sea

Stop living blindly, hear what I say

Stand up, don't walk away

A revolution is coming soon

The children today can't be fooled

I know this world is smaller now

Don't ignore this simple truth

The sea is not one giant farm

Tell me where now can I roam, I roam

Tell me where now is my home, my wilderness home

Tell me where now I can go to hear the song of the sea

So free the dolphins, save the whales

And breezes will fill up your sails

Love the land, love the seas

Love Mother Earth, won't you please

I know I'm feeling stronger now

Heed the simple truth

The sea is not one giant farm

Tell me where now can I roam, I roam

Tell me where now is my home, my wilderness home

Tell me where now can I roam, I roam

Tell me where now is my home, my wilderness home

Tell me where now I can go to hear the song of the sea

—*Les Stroud*

ACKNOWLEDGMENTS

I would like to acknowledge Wendy Turner, Barry Farrell, and my team, my crew, my staff, and my friends on the road and in the edit suites and offices—both past and present. They have been with me through some crazy adventures. We have laughed and argued and scratched our heads. We have sweated and frozen. We have slept on airport floors using our suitcases for pillows. We've eaten crap food and dined on awesome meals. We have puked and caught malaria (sorry, Andrew and Dan). We have scaled mountains and stood and breathed looking out on the beautiful Andes. We have connected with remote primitive-living peoples in touching and meaningful ways, and we have been screwed over by losers trying to hold us hostage for more money. And those in the office have worked 48 straight hours of editing shifts and had to redo all manner of work based on some new whim of mine.

Through it all, these friends acquiesced to my stubborn antics and narcissistic ways. They have suggested fantastic creative ideas that worked and made "my" job so much better. They don't hang on waiting for the ratings to come in—they simply hang on waiting for the final edit, wanting to know it's a solid show with a high standard of creativity. They may leave me alone to do my thing on *Survivorman* but I know they are out there supporting me, and without them I could never have continued to do it. For *Beyond Survival* they took a lot of the lumps with me and kept on pushing through. I won't name them all here. You know who you are.

I want to thank Laura Bombier. Without her, this book simply would not have been possible. I love her tenacious creative work in the field on every shoot I have done since the second season of *Survivorman*, and I love her amazing photography and creative design skills for this book. We have been partners through thick, through thin, and through sleeping on rooster-poop-covered floors and in jungle huts. She is an artistic genius. She has been my creative partner, my toughest critic, my greatest supporter, my lover, and my friend, and we have done and seen more in a few years than most people do and see in a lifetime.

My life is not complete without my son, Logan, and my daughter, Raylan, who have paid the highest price for my lifestyle, which is so focused on my need to create and to pursue adventure. I love you both, and it is always my highest thrill when you can, on occasion, join me on these crazy journeys and other adventures.

Special thanks to Bill Thomas, Charlie Lambe, Nat Quansa, Jackie Bobrowsky, Delia Ackerman, Jim Yost, Dave Reid, Anton Roberts, Barry Clark, Jason Schoonover, Chrystelle Hadjikakou, Ben Larrive, Peter Esteves, Johnny Askwith, Andrew Sheppard, Drew Carnwath, Dan Reynolds, Bryan Potvin, Kate Heming, Rob Evis, Barry Clark. And thanks to Elizabeth Jenkins, who penned the books *The Return of the Inka* and *Journey to Q'eros: Golden Cradle of the Inka*.

Lastly, my heartfelt thanks continue to go out to Brad Wilson, Kelly Hope, and Noelle Zitzer of Harper-Collins for their continued support and interest in my writings; and to my lawyer, David Dembroski, who continues to laugh every time I say this is the last time.